PARENTING ACROSS THE DIGITAL DIVIDE

A National Conversation on the Impact of Technology and Media on Our Families

Dr. Helen Boehm

authorHOUSE®

AuthorHouse™
1663 Liberty Drive
Bloomington, IN 47403
www.authorhouse.com
Phone: 1 (800) 839-8640

Published by AuthorHouse 01/15/2018

ISBN: 978-1-5462-2397-9 (sc)
ISBN: 978-1-5462-2446-4 (e)

Print information available on the last page.

"Careful the things you say, children will listen.

Careful the things you do, children will see and learn."

Steven Sondheim
Into the Woods

CONTENTS

INTRODUCTION

It has been said that if you live at the ocean's edge, you can either build a fence around your house or you can teach your kids how to swim. We certainly cannot prevent our children from interacting with the tech-focused world into which they were born. Nor would we want to exclude them from the amazing opportunities that innovation and connectivity now provide. Today's families are, however, concerned about the impact of Internet technology on their children and ready to confront an increasingly problematic media landscape. We want our kids to embrace the challenges that await them, ensure their safe futures – and, teach them how to swim!

As a psychologist working in the children's entertainment industry for over thirty years, I've spent a lot of time watching what your children have been watching. As I've overseen programming and advertising in the kids' media space move from broadcast TV to cable, digital and wireless distribution, I have witnessed the unprecedented growth and influence of the Internet in all aspects of teaching, learning and entertainment.

My purpose for doing this book is to open a dialogue with parents to gain a deeper understanding of the Internet and its effects upon their children's behavior. I hope to shine a light upon the impact of digital exposure to the modeling of pro- and anti-social behavior, the blurring of fantasy and reality, the virtual victimization of youngsters and the *sexualization* and *pornification* of the media.

In an environment saturated with technology, bombarding images and interactivity, we need to pause and examine what makes our kids tick...and, click! We cannot just build a fence around our children. We need to model emotional resilience and build support for the 21st century skills that will enable our kids to swim - and thrive - in a digital world.

THE DIGITAL DIVIDE

We did not grow up on the same side of the digital divide as did the offspring we welcomed into to the world and have nurtured for the past two decades. Parents may be comfortable on one side, but on the other side of the divide sits post-millennial youngsters who have never known a time without social media or that the Amazon (without the .com) is a river in South America. They use google as a verb and don't remember when MTV only played music videos. They are affectionately known as Digital Natives, Post-Millennials, GenZ and iGen. If you ask them where they live, they will answer, "On the Internet."

Straddling this digital divide are the iconic iPhone and iPad, giving rise to the sea change that has now defined the distinct neurological wiring differences between generations. The original side of touch-screen technology included high tech toys and personal digital assistants (PDAs) like Palm Pilots and Newtons. The introduction of the Apple iPad on April 3, 2010, however, put digital tools and portals to knowledge on the new side of the digital divide and literally, into the hands of babes. Remarkably, toddlers, unable to operate a computer mouse, could use their fists and fingers to swipe, touch and open icons on tablets! Now, a new generation of our youngest children are empowered to discover new worlds of information and live (where else?) on the Internet.

If you have ever witnessed a baby swatting a picture in a magazine trying to reveal what's behind it, or stroking an image on a TV screen, wondering why it won't open, it's easy to be completely awestruck by the power of this technology and the absolute wonder of their intent. Our youngest post-millennials now have the astounding ability to interact with technology and create a dynamic dialogue. It is *open sesame* with some 21st century magic sprinkled on top. "Pat the Bunny" - or anything else - and you're on the net!

Screens may be second only to parents as the most potent socializing agent of our culture. As children Skype with grandparents, build robots and plug into all things digital, we can only hold our collective breath regarding the effects of media exposure, both positive and negative, that await them. Even the most caring and careful parents; attentive to the selection of age-appropriate Internet apps, rating software, bullying blockers and safety browsers could not have anticipated the tsunami of content that would be available to their kids, simply for the asking on the World Wide Web.

Since the introduction of the iPad, colorful touchscreens have become the most favored playthings for toddlers. With the same little hand a child uses to explore her three-dimensional universe, she is able to singlehandedly unlock a world of information pathways and learning adventures. So, as kids interact with technology, parents must responsibly provide guidance and protection, as well as model appropriate behaviors and become involved in content choices. Sounds overwhelming, and it – almost - is!

Evaluating the risks and opportunities that an increasingly connected world presents will forever be a daunting task. At every age and stage of a child's development, new challenges and vulnerabilities, with respect to tech, will appear. Those of us with children and grandchildren find comfort in the familiar phrase, "parenting is not a sprint... it's a long distance run," because of the challenges that will continue to confront us, daily. Mindful of the famous 3C's: connectivity, communication and content, our youngest kids will follow our lead into a digital environment where results are instantaneous and gratification is immediate.

The World Wide Web is vast and known for its anonymity and reach. Along with the sheer volume of adult content on the web, the Internet poses tricky navigational issues. It's impossible to quantify the amount of inappropriate images our post-millennial children will ultimately access on-line. Let's just say, it's a lot! And, with the proliferation of mobile and portable devises, these numbers expand exponentially; to beyond anything most of us can even comprehend.

Of course, the virtual life affords numerous perks and opportunities as well as difficulties. You can be invisible, invent a new identity, interact with complete anonymity, and on and on. You can enter a chat room and reveal anything you want, without even being yourself, or fly a plane without leaving the safety of the couch in your den. Certainly, stepping into the unknown can be as exhilarating as it is scary. If you're reading this book on-line, you have already crossed over the digital divide. Welcome to the new normal!

When it comes to products for kids, today, almost everything - from the space between the slats of a crib, flame retardants in pajamas and paints used on toys - are regulated for safety. Luckily, most items children use include some government oversight or association standards for keeping kids safe. However, extremely careful parents, attentive to everything their children are seeing, hearing and learning, find there are few safe spaces on the World Wide Web.

PARENT AS ADVOCATE

The role that parents play in mediating children's Internet exposure, while shaping their ethical and critical thinking skills, is indispensable. In reality, kids may encounter scary images, sexually explicit material, hear hateful speech or see violent acts performed, and you can be fairly sure that the Internet is the likely culprit. So, it is probably not a matter of *if* your digital native will stumble upon unsuitable content on the web - only when.

It's time for all of us to expand our understanding of post-millennials, whose comfort and connection with the virtual world is far more developed than our own (or than any other generation that preceded them!) The game-changing role that Internet access, available 24-7 in your pocket or under your pillow, has brought to the process of parenting is astounding.

Almost every aspect of our communication and socialization is now influenced by a computer or telephone screen. With so many unsuitable messages and images in this virtual sphere, we absolutely must parent smarter and safer. Throughout this book, we'll discuss ways to do just that. We'll examine the impact of the continuous connection to mobile screens on our GenZ kids, with an emphasis on the Internet's effect on adolescents and teens. We'll discuss topics, including:

- The modeling of behavior, including contagion and teen suicide
- Virtual victimization and kids' blurring of reality and fantasy
- The impact of the news on our families and what kids are actually worrying about
- The sexualization of the kids' culture and how parents can have impact
- Effects of the net from eating disorders to sexting and cyberbullying, and
- Addiction; a reality of the interaction with net-based gaming, cybersex and porn

SAFEGUARDING KIDS ON THE NET

The flight attendant holds up a plastic oxygen mask for everyone on the plane to see. If the aircraft's cabin should lose pressure during flight, she explains, the mask will drop down in front of you. But then she adds an ominous warning to people traveling with kids, "Secure the oxygen mask over *your* nose first – before securing the mask of your child." Indeed a metaphor and rallying cry for families facing new digital challenges and a future filled with exciting, yet uncertain, new technologies. In order to ensure the safety of children and prepare and empower them for the future, parents must become knowledgeable, *themselves*, about the opportunities -- and the risks -- their kids will encounter in a networked world. Parents need to educate themselves and provide a family friendly foundation for their connected homes and digital natives.

Importantly, parenting smarter requires those who care for and about kids minimize the specific risks they will encounter in this new wired world. Emerging technologies from smart devises for home-alone security, jewelry allowing for constant communication and location monitoring, to connected toys and appliances that will order your groceries, play music you love and even teach your kids manners, are the new underpinnings of modern family life. But, as these devices collect data, interact with your children and lead them on to the Internet, they will need *your* protection and guidance. Becoming familiar with the apps and websites that your kids visit, will help you better guide and support them. You would never allow your young child to roam alone around a public park. But, on the net, your child is navigating a complicated and often, dimly-lit, park. Here, they should not turn to Siri and Alexa. They should turn to you.

There are numerous content filters, blockers and web interfaces that offer "pockets of protection," for young tech users. Along with careful monitoring and parental oversight, these devises are helpful, but not, completely, foolproof. By junior high school, many Gen Z digital experts can navigate around some of the most robust new filters and controls. The best solution, therefore, is probably not more sophisticated Internet blocking gadgets, but exploring digital literacy and the importance of empathy, self-discipline and personal responsibility with your growing kids.

> *NOTE TO PARENTS*: You will find some of the best and most practical advice *about* the Internet *on* the Internet!

Set clear guidelines with your kids and monitor their on-line activity. Certainly, parents cannot prevent every circumstance where a child may stumble upon inappropriate material on the net, but we can certainly be attentive and manage the risk.

Stephen Balkam, Founder & CEO of The Family Online Safety Institute (FOSI.org), offers excellent advice to parents. His world view is a good place to start.

7 Steps to Good Digital Parenting:

https://www.fosi.org

> 1. **Talk with your kids**
>
> It sounds simple, but the number one indicator of good digital parenting is keeping an open line of communication going with your kids. Talk early and often. It is not like the birds and the bees discussion. It is more like an ongoing dialogue that will move and shift as your child works her way through several key developmental stages. Stay calm. Be open and direct. But keep talking.
>
> 2. **Educate yourself**
>
> This is probably the first technology in human history where the kids are leading the adults. It is very humbling to have a 7 year old explain how to upload a video. Or your teen rolling his eyes once again as you try to master Pandora. But there is a wealth of tips, videos, explanations and guides out there. If in doubt, simply type in your question or concern in your favorite search engine and there will be more than enough information to go on.
>
> 3. **Use parental controls**
>
> It goes without saying that there is content on the Internet you don't want your kids stumbling upon. All of the major operating systems, search engines, cell phone providers and gaming platforms provide either free or inexpensive parental controls to help you manage your kids' online experience. And, as your kids get older, move from controls to monitoring tools
>
> 4. **Set ground rules & apply sanctions**
>
> Many parents don't know where to start in creating rules of the road for their kids' digital use. But there are many online safety contracts to choose from as well as simple house rules such as no devices at dinner and handing in their phones at night. Once you've set the rules, enforce them. Let your kids know that they will lose

online privileges if they break the rules and be clear and consistent about what those sanctions will be.

5. Friend and follow, but don't stalk

When your teen opens her Facebook account at 13, ensure you're her first friend. Follow your kids on Twitter and YouTube. But don't be tempted to spy on your kids, either. Talking instead of stalking is what builds trust. Give your teen some space to experiment, to take (healthy) risks and to build resiliency.

6. Explore, share and celebrate

With the rules and tools in place, don't forget to just go online with your kids. Play games, watch videos, share photos and generally hang out with your children online. Learn from them and have fun. Share your favorite sites and download their apps. See the world through their eyes. And let them know your values and beliefs as you guide them on their way.

7. Be a good digital role model

Be the change you want to see in your kids. Keep an eye on your own digital habits and compulsions and model good digital behavior and balance. Your kids will pay far more attention to what you do, than to what you say – both online and offline.

WHEN IS TOO SOON? AND HOW MUCH IS TOO MUCH?

Digital learning starts with the very first swipe. Very young children seem pre-wired and predisposed to interact with new technology. Ask any mom who has used an iPhone, successfully, to distract a fussy 2 -year-old, and she will tell you that there's tech in her child's DNA. But, before introducing the latest baby-tech gadget, it's important to determine your family's digital comfort level, the quantity of screen time you're considering for your child and how time spent with technology might displace other valuable play, social learning and skill-building opportunities.

Parents want specific answers to questions regarding the timing of appropriate digital experiences for their kids. Unfortunately, there are no scientifically determined dates, times or ages to share with you, only some child development indications and a little common sense. We know that from the first days of life, babies connect the immediate gratification of making something happen -- *with* a rewarding outcome. Their responsiveness and engagement encourages greater examination. This continuous cause and effect connection is the absolute basis of early learning and, at the appropriate time, can be significantly buoyed by technology.

The American Academy of Pediatrics (AAP) recommends that children under 18 months of age avoid all tablets, TV's and screens. Research has shown that babies have a "video deficit" and do not adequately process information delivered on a 2-dimensional screen. Around 2 years of age, the Academy acknowledges and accepts kids' desire to participate in the digital culture on a limited basis. They advise no more than one hour per day of high quality educational programming with parents co-viewing alongside their kids.

Importantly, the AAP discourages background television for adults whenever young kids are in the same room. Adults speak to children less when the television is on and this lack of verbal interaction is thought to interfere with overall language acquisition and cognitive processing. Pediatricians also advise parents to put away the tablets, turn off the TV and sit down and play with their kids, when it is possible. This may not always be easy or convenient, but the value of one-to-one interaction and bonding cannot be overstated.

Without comparison, the capacity of touch-screen technology to excite and delight very young kids is an extraordinary thing to watch. Toddlers who are developing fine motor control around their index fingers can now deliberately press an icon on a screen and receive immediate feedback. Good apps, shows and interactive experiences for preschoolers take into account the young child's currently developing abilities. A developmentally appropriate interface can encourage a positive and lasting educational experience. Reinforced by well-constructed apps that are varied in pace and suitable to a child's cognitive development, great preschool education has gone tech.

Beginning interactive experiences should not frustrate kids - or their parents - but always be fun and culminate in success. If collaborative play is built on a narrative, stories should be linear and simple, with a beginning, middle and end. The AAP encourages families to create personalized media plans and their own guidelines for healthy levels of digital screen interaction.

NOTE TO PARENTS ON YOUR YOUNG CHILD'S INTRODUCTION TO THE DIGITAL WORLD:

There are excellent web resources to help introduce and guide young children through the challenges of the evolving digital realm. The National Association for the Education of Young Children (NAEYC.org), is a professional organization comprised of early-childhood educators. Its website offers parents, as well as early childhood educators, the latest information and advice regarding children's earliest technology tools and appropriate media choices. In addition, Public Broadcasting's Parenting Website, (PBS PARENTS.org), is a web-based child development and early-learning resource offering great tips for parents on the best of digital learning materials and age-appropriate video programming.

DIGITAL SAFETY

Surely, there is no role as important as that of a parent, nor responsibility as profound as the safety and well-being of one's family. Now, with all the talk about safe spaces, one can no longer assume that a child's bedroom, the school gym, the church basement or grandma's kitchen are totally safe and protected. Because as long as your child has access to webcams, iPhone apps and even certain connected toys, safety is *not* a given. Parents are the first line of defense in all areas of child protection. Our responsibility is to enable our kids to share in all the opportunities and benefits that the digital world has to offer, while at the same time ensuring their safety and privacy. This task is challenging -- while barreling down the information super highway or staying safe in your own living room.

The safeguarding of children is every parent's #1 priority and concerned families and communities want to know best practices for accomplishing this. A sensible community perspective is necessary, as well as a candid look at which web-based content parents can control, and which they, realistically, cannot. From the disclosure of credit card information to distribution of selfies, we need to guide and protect kids in both the physical and on-line worlds in which they live. Long term dedication and care are required to secure a safe virtual environment, while balancing technology's risks and rewards.

We know that all the Spector Pro and Net Nanny services offered to protect very young children will never be able to compete with our kids' desire for popularity over privacy. Parenting today involves an entire new set of mentoring tools. In this emerging world of the famous 3C's; connectivity, communication and content, we are raising families in a digital environment where results are personalized and gratification is immediate. Still, parents play a critical advisory role in shaping the social, emotional and critical thinking skills that will support their kids in the future.

DIGITAL LITERACY

Fostering digital literacy does not require your understanding of sophisticated tech equipment or the functioning of the oxygen system of an airplane. It simply necessitates a continuing conversation at your kitchen table that begins when your 2-year-old wants to play with your iPhone. Becoming digitally literate requires a flexibility and readiness to develop new strategies for discovering and experiencing content. The ability to locate and integrate information collected from multiple sources is a central theme of digital literacy competency. However, it is the ability to apply this knowledge that will truly enable our kids to become far more digitally literate than their parents will ever be.

From TV to the Internet and across all forms of media, being well informed requires updated information and an open minded approach. Surely, the word "update" is the cornerstone of this new literacy movement. Digital literacy also includes a comfort with technology tools that are, themselves, in a constant state of improvement and advancement. One must be literate in the moment, as well as available to life-long learning in an ever evolving technology landscape.

DIGITAL REPUTATION

When Harvard College rescinded offers of admissions to about a dozen incoming freshman for posting insensitive statements about minorities and sexually explicit messages on a private group chat site, shocked parents asked, "Can they really do that?" Apparently, the answer is yes, the university can and, it did! A lesson for parents, kids and families, that in the connected world in which we now live, one's digital footprint and ultimate digital reputation is forever.

The disappointed parents and the humiliated kids who were denied membership in the Class of 2021 protested this harsh punishment, which, they argued, violated their right to free speech and Internet privacy. But, the university argued that it had the responsibility to revoke an offer of admission if it learned of behavior reflecting unacceptable moral character -- in virtual *or* real life.

College admissions staffs, police officers, coaches and potential employers are among the selection authorities interested in your child's digital reputation. They know that there will always be posts, videos, messages and photographs that "come back to haunt" and embarrassing content that simply never goes away. Realistically, there will probably be future opportunities, friendships and scholarships which will result in disappointment and pre-judgement because of material that has made its way on to the World Wide Web. Balancing our family's on-line interaction and outreach is critically important, regardless of the immediate appropriateness or context that we think provides a justification.

On-line safety, the significance of our children's virtual footprints and the importance of their digital reputations encourage parents to be proactive in the digital lives of their families. The Internet is a window into an ever widening world that opens early and with ease. Be it a nursery monitor, interactive video game or virtual violin lesson, personal data is constantly being monitored and captured. As connected digital citizens we want our digital natives to be safe. Their footprint will be their brand for a very long time and will be comprised of almost all the chats, photos, posts and words they have ever shared with others on the Internet.

MONKEY SEE, MONKEY DO...
MODELING BEHAVIOR

Robert McCloskey's charming children's book, "Make Way for Ducklings," finds Mother Mallard teaching her ducklings everything they need to know about growing up to be ducks. By patterning by example or "imprinting," she teaches her young to waddle, swim in-line and copy her every move. Children adore learning about how the ducklings learn. And, just like the ducklings, copying and mimicking their own parents' behavior, human children begin their own continuous social learning process into adulthood.

The work of psychologist Albert Bandura expands the example of ducklings and applies these patterns to how human children learn. His social learning theory explains how kids model behavior, something with significant implications for studying the effects of digital exposure. According to Bandura's theory, infants are born with the instinctive desire to imitate adult behavior and pattern their actions on the behavior of parents and other close adults. Not unlike ducklings parading behind their mother, children "follow the leader." The imprinting of behavior is the preferred human learning style.

Chicks and ducklings are also known to copy the behavior of the first moving object they see, immediately upon being hatched. So, they will imprint a rolling ball or a human being, and then follow along in a neat, straight line. Bandura also noted that, like ducklings, human children's role models need not be human. Children will mimic and follow cartoon characters, animals or other fantasy creatures. Humans will model those behaviors that produce the most pleasure and that will result in the most favorable consequences. You will often see two year-olds "copying" the movements of a frog or a favorite animated character.

Behavioral patterns are also reinforced when a close role model is rewarded for an action. It's interesting to notice that when a behavioral model is continuously acknowledged and reinforced, children will internalize the acceptability of their actions. Over time, in fact, the young observer will likely integrate aspects of this model into his or her own behavior. Watching a cartoon character being constantly rewarded with candy or reinforced with friendship, for being polite, for example, can influence a child to become more polite. Unfortunately, the negative holds true, as well. Although I don't recommend the constant candy rewards, it's important to realize that this modeling is occurring all the time. And, much of the modeling is virtual, not, necessarily, something the child experiences directly.

Social learning theory – and your mother – tell us that we learn how to parent by being parented. We watch our parents carefully and reinforce those behaviors practicing with our dolls, pets and siblings. We pattern our behavior on the examples close to us, modeling appropriate actions and testing what feels right and appropriate. Usually, nuanced rewards - from glances of approval to nods and smiles – help us determine if we're doing it right.

Life-long behavioral training is constantly taking place and eventually defines our personalities and our behavior. It's the comportment we experience at the kitchen table and the schoolyard. But, increasingly, those observations and learning experiences also extend to reality TV, YouTube and the videos that digital natives watch on the web.

A strong, personal revelation of the power of images to resonate and model behavior in the minds of youngsters came my first day on the job at MTV Networks. It was the 1990's and I was hired as the Senior Vice President for Public Responsibility and Network Standards (or perhaps, more accurately, the "chief censor"), at the Viacom owned youth-oriented cable network. As a psychologist, my prior position was to oversee the impact of media on the attitudes and behaviors of young people at the Fox Television Network, so I was prepared to help music and programming producers meet broadcast standards. I was also hired to "put out some fires," but, what I never imagined was that one of those fires would be one, literally, set by a 5-year-old boy, attempting to imitate an incident he saw on an MTV cartoon.

Replicating the fantasy antics of the animated Beavis and Butthead cartoon series, the youngster said he tried to "copy" his heroes with dreadful consequences. The child set a fire that engulfed the trailer home where he and his family lived. His 2-year-old sister tragically died in that fire.

Millions of viewers watched the same adult-oriented evening episode of that animated comedy satire and, seemingly, remained unaffected by it. It was never intended for children to see and it was broadcast in the evening. But, even though it was not targeted to kids or intended to be viewed by them, one young child was horrifically impacted by it. And, that is one child too many.

This was, perhaps, a perfect storm comprised of an isolated instance of not predicting a potential digital association and action and a missed opportunity for better home safety, parental oversight and supervision. But, the lesson for parents back then and now is that images have significant and often unintended impact. Whether delivered by TV, tablet, computer screen or phone, images can affect who we are and who we become. In addition, we understand the exceptional status that cartoon characters carry in the culture of children. And, since kids quickly pattern and are easily influenced, the vigilance of parents and caring adults is critical. Even innocent images can, unfortunately, have unforeseen effects.

*NOTE TO PARENTS ON MODELING BEHAVIOR:*Kids are constantly watching, copying and mimicking adult behavior. Since we know that kids learn spontaneously, through observation and imitation, we may want to carefully examine our own behaviors as we interact with media and the net. If you are attached to your phone and distracted by constant media around you, chances are that your child will be tethered to technology as well. Family media use is a strong predictor of your child's eventual media habits. Parents' excessive use of mobile devices is associated with fewer verbal interactions between parents and kids and may result in a child's inability to gain what she considers to be, adequate parental attention.

Caroline Knorr has sage advice for parents about setting appropriate examples of media usage on Common Sense Media (CommonSenseMedia.org)

Be a Role Model - Find a Healthy Balance with Media and Technology:

https://www.commonsensemedia.org

"We've all seen that dad yakking away on his cell phone at the playground while his 3-year-old resorts to increasingly desperate measures to get his attention. We've also been that parent. We answer emails, update Facebook, take a conference call, and try to get in that one last text. The thing is, kids notice -- and they're not happy about it.

Lots of studies address the impact of screen time on kids, and guidelines show how much is appropriate at what age. But researchers are just beginning to look into the effect that parents' screen use has on kids. A Boston Medical Center study of how families at a restaurant interacted with each other when they used cell phones demonstrated that caregivers who were "highly absorbed" in their devices responded harshly to their kids' bids for attention. And in her book The Big Disconnect: Protecting Childhood and Family Relationships in the Digital Age, Catherine Steiner-Adair found that kids often feel they have to compete with devices for their parents' attention.

Most importantly, kids learn their screen habits from us. It might be easier if someone just gave parents a recommended daily time limit so we'd know when to stop. In the meantime, we'll need to find balance. But there's a huge motivator to change our behavior: The little girl on the play structure, the boy learning to skateboard, the twins playing dress-up. They're watching us, watching our phones.

5 Ways to Find a Healthy Balance of Media and Technology

1. **Be a role model.** When kids are around, set an example by using media the way you want them to use it. Keep mobile devices away from the dinner table (learn about our Device-Free Dinner initiative), turn the TV off when it's not being watched, and use a DVR to record shows to watch later.

2. **Start good habits early.** The secret to healthy media use is to establish time limits and stick to them. Start when your kids are young by setting screen limits that work for your family's needs and schedule. And don't just talk the talk -- walk the walk!

3. **Use media together.** Whenever you can, watch, play, and listen with your kids. Ask them what they think of the content. Share your values, and help kids relate what they learn in the media to events and other activities in which they're involved. With older kids, you can draw them out by sharing stuff from your Facebook and Instagram accounts.

4. **Keep distractions to a minimum.** You probably tell your kids to turn their phones off during homework time. Get rid of the stuff that distracts you, too. Hide your apps so they don't display, set your phone to "do not disturb," or shut down your devices during important family time.

5. **Turn off work.** Many parents feel they need to be constantly accessible to their jobs. But that's stressful, frustrating, and not realistic. Set boundaries for work time and family time."

RISKY BUSINESS

Every aspect of our communication, work and socialization is now influenced by technology. Screens place us at our favorite vacation destinations, allow us to see our pets play at day care and deliver our favorite entertainment. The ubiquitous Internet provides our families with opportunities for learning, communication and incomparable benefits. With so many rewards, we need a coordinated approach and a broad range of strategies to protect and harvest these contributions. Parents are, of course, the first line of defense in all areas of child protection. They are the basic building blocks of their children's school and life success.

The safeguarding of children must become a family and community priority. Long term dedication and care are required to secure a safe virtual environment for all kids at all ages and stages of development. There is no silver bullet for controlling the risks technology will present to our families in the future. But, removing the Internet and digital communications from our daily lives is as unrealistic as it is impractical. For better or worse, the Internet is here... and here to stay!

There are few things that make you feel as strongly connected to part of a community as the activities and interactivity on the Internet. The net is "Triple A" -- accessible, affordable and anonymous. It's available to everyone without entrance fees, permission slips or credit cards. It has changed the way we process information and moves virtual knowledge into our primary realm of experience by a tap on a devise.

For those of us who need to watch television in order to sleep or need to get weather updates or football scores on our phones, our personal technology has been transformed from a helpful appendage to an integral aspect of who we are. Digital literacy experts agree that the Internet has become a critical element of our personalities and our identities. Our interaction with, and on the Internet, rivals relationships with our other primary drivers: food, clothing and shelter. Technology and the Internet have impacted the way we process information, socialize, pray, shop and parent.

It's ironic that our digital passions have contributed to our dependence on the very same wireless devices that were supposed to free us up and boost our independence. Of particular concern for us and our families is the generalized anxiety that just having these devises may foster. What if we were to lose our phones? Or, the anticipation that if something terrible were to happen, is it possible that we wouldn't know about it right away? What would happen if we couldn't get a text or a call? Estimates are that, on average, we are checking our smartphones over 200 times per day. This rallies us into a state of hypervigilance and commands our central nervous systems to remain alert. This fight or flight readiness mode is an intergenerational phenomenon now shared by GenZ, their parents and their grandparents.

Parents must be smart about the digital lives their children lead and should appreciate the fact that their own on-line world will probably never attain the digital fluency their GenZ kids enjoy. But, that doesn't mean that they can't help their children achieve a balance in their non-virtual vs. screen-time usage, control of their stress and tech overload and their acquisition of those important "netiquette" skills. I would encourage conversations with your children about *why* you are limiting and guiding screen access for all members of your family. This may mean more Lego instead of Minecraft; family game night instead of iPads and, perhaps, a walk in nature instead of watching the Nature Channel. Dinner without TV or other electronic devices nearby may seem challenging, but it's interesting to note that Steve Jobs had tech-free dinners with his own kids. It's not necessary to deny the existence of media and personal tech devises, just minimize their presence, their impact and their risks.

Parenting in the Internet age is frustrating and protecting kids has become increasingly more difficult. Certainly, we cannot prevent every circumstance where a child may stumble upon inappropriate material on the Internet, so we should focus on trying to minimize and mitigate these potential experiences. Obviously, as kids get older, oversight of the net becomes even more challenging. There was a time when safe-browsing software could be installed on the family PC, which the family would share in the living room. But, thanks to the proliferation of phones, laptops and tablets, this strategy is no longer effective for the many post-millennials who are usually more tech savvy than their parents.

Parental controls, privacy settings and some nanny-software have their time and place in a young child's life. Many of these programs are helpful and provide "pockets of protection" for younger children. But, how does a parent ever compete with disappearing texts sent on sent through apps and platforms with names like Wicr, Hash and StealthChat?

Be careful not to totally rely on a software solution to shelter your child from inappropriate content on-line. A comprehensive digital safety net requires continuous parental monitoring and supervision. There are numerous suggestions for keeping kids safe on blogs and websites, for example, you can enable YouTube Safety Mode on web browsers and pre-program time spent on-line or playing video games.

Your children may be cyber-smart and super savvy. But, that does not preclude the critical role that you will continue to play in shaping their values and critical thinking skills, as well as intervening when your assistance and maturity is needed. And, even if you can't control or restrict the digital universe of your tweens and teens, you can focus your efforts on managing, monitoring and helping to guide their behavior. Even with all the latest tech gadgets, you are, and will always be, the most powerful and influential teacher in your child's life. So, in addition to the important safety "netiquette" below, model the behavior you would like to see reflected in your digital citizen of tomorrow.

NOTE TO PARENTS ABOUT ON-LINE RISKS: What is the "netiquette" of on-line behavior that will keep kids appropriately engaged, but will also keep them out of harm's way? The WIREDSAFETY (WIREDSAFETY.com) website provides information, education and great resources about privacy, safety and responsible Internet use. Parry Aftab, the organization's founder, has advice for minimizing kids' risks on the net.

Netiquette's Big No-No's:

http://www.wiredsafety.com

> "• Flaming—inciting or provoking an argument.
>
> • Posting false information about someone else.
>
> • Using someone's account without their okay.
>
> • Using someone's password (even if they gave it to you) without their okay
>
> • Sending a large attachment without asking first..

- Referring to someone by their real name online if they want to remain anonymous in public.

- Posting personal information about someone else without their okay.

- Talking off-topic in a special topic chatroom.

- Posting a pic of someone without asking first.

- Giving out someone's screen name or e-mail without their okay"

BLURRING OF FANTASY AND REALITY

Screens have been the uninvited guests in American homes for decades, so how has the change in the playing field sparked new debate? After all, we saw Roadrunner jump off cliffs and get squished by bulldozers. We saw nudity in films and heard sexual banter on late night TV. Full frontal nudity filled the pages of magazines from National Geographic to Playboy. But, unlike kids today, past generations were rarely considered at risk for serious psychological or emotional problems because of their exposure to media. If we did see something that we probably shouldn't have seen, it rarely had a life-changing effect. There was little concern that our fleeting exposure to inappropriate content would have any long lasting psychological consequences. How then, have risks escalated so much and media's potential negative impact become so troubling?

Media operates and educates 24/7. Although it is certainly worthwhile to minimize the risks of exposure to violent and anti-social images, it is just the beginning of ensuring your child's safety. Even under-the covers, in the gym and during meal time, phone screens and videos are close at hand, ready to influence, socialize and even comfort. If the ubiquity of screens and imagery were not enough to answer the question, "Why is the media more dangerous, now?" sophisticated visual effects, ultra-realistic visions and amazing high definition techniques certainly come into play to make screen time more potent than ever. Today, images are more realistic and can also be more terrifying than ever before. Visual effects and new computer-assisted graphics continue to raise the bar in making the fantastical look real, and the realistic seem like you are actually there.

Parents need not wait for the evidence to be published before helping their iGen kids understand the important distinction between what is real and what is not. In addition to more explicit and racy content, the impact of large screens, computer screens, smart phones and tablets on the developing brain is formidable. As we examine the cognitive consequences of virtual input on the development of digital natives, we must be alert to the fact that images based on virtual and real content may be processed by us in identical ways.

It's tough enough for adults to separate what they've seen, virtually, from what they have actually experienced. A growing body of research indicates that children whose memories of actual and virtual events are often blurred grow up to indistinguishable memories of each. And, in a world of reality TV the confusion is only extended. The line between what's real and what is not can be so blurry that we must assume that as children learn, virtual experiences may be integrated into their thought processes as *actual experiences*. Therefore, when a child's scary dream or fear requires a caring adult to explain the difference between real and make believe, it is clear that young kids need a great deal of parenting assistance and loving kindness.

The intensity, realism and repetition of the Internet, along with the ease of bypassing watchdogs and filters to reach directly into our home computers, phones and TV's pose new problems for families. How can we monitor the content being streamed directly into our child's iPad? And, how do we handle the fear and anxiety that is so prevalent in today's media messaging?

Growing up in the era before amazing special effects, I remember always looking for the hidden wires that enabled Superman, Mary Poppins and Peter Pan to fly. The wires usually looked more like thick ropes which you could see in the shadows - a dead give-away, along with the bulge of the harness around the actor's waist, that the pretend factor was in play. There was a clarity to real vs. make believe that was often a relief, especially when things got scary. But without low tech comparisons, Gen Z kids, are as susceptible to the impact of screen images as real-life events.

Research substantiates parents' observations that, chemically, a young child's initial response to on-screen and real-life frights are pretty much equivalent. Both methods of stimulation cause a rise in the fight or flight chemical production in the brain. Although the linkages of intense screen effects and children's emotional reactions are not a new phenomenon, the uptick in the "startled effect" affecting children so frequently has reframed the kids' screen debate.

As parents seek to understand every movie rating for a film their post-millennials want to see, they quickly learn that they will never achieve a similar fail-safe level of comfort over the content on their mobile screens.

NOTE TO PARENTS ABOUT HELPING KIDS DIFFERENTIATE FANTASY FROM REALITY: I cannot adequately stress the importance of co-viewing entertainment media with youngsters and reinforcing the difference between fantasy and reality in all forms of entertainment and advertising. Common Sense Media's (CommonSenseMedia.org) Caroline Knorr offers valuable tips for media partnering between kids and parents, from mobile screen time to modeling healthy habits.

Dr. Helen Boehm

New Healthy Media Habits for Young Kids:

https://www.commonsensemedia.org

Choose the good stuff (and not too much!). When your kids ask to see, play, or download something, don't just take their word for it -- check up on it. A lot of the age recommendations on media products are the creators' best guess and aren't necessarily a match for your child's age and developmental stage. Read product reviews from independent sources (like Common Sense Media). Say no if you're not comfortable with it. And when you approve something, help your kids enjoy it along with their other activities.

Don't use screens right before bed, and keep them out of the bedroom overnight. Kids really need their sleep. Screens in the bedroom -- especially in the hour before bedtime -- interfere with the entire process of winding down, preparing for rest, and waking up refreshed and ready to tackle the day. If you're unable to make the bedroom a screen-free zone (which is optimal but not always possible), keep TVs off for at least an hour before bedtime and set tablets or phones to night mode, turn off any notifications, and/ or consider using Guided Access or another device setting to keep phones/tablets locked on a music or an alarm clock app.

Turn off the TV if no one is watching it. A lot of parents of young kids keep the TV on for company. But so-called background TV has been shown to get in the way of parents talking and interacting with their kids -- which are key to helping kids learn language and communication. Background TV can also expose kids to age-inappropriate content. Seek out other forms of entertainment that you can listen to with your kid, such as music, kids' podcasts, and audiobooks.

Make time for enjoying media with your kids, especially reading. Reading to your kid is one of the best things you can do -- period. It's great for bonding, but it also sets the stage for learning. While it's nice to have a little library of books at home, you can read whatever's available and it'll be good for them. Product labels, signs, packaging copy -- anything with words is fine. If you're raising your kid in a place where you don't completely know the language, feel free to read books or articles to them in your native tongue. Or just make up stories -- it's the rhythm, sounds, and communication that are important for kids to hear.

Practice what you preach. Remember, your kids are watching you. When your kids are little, create a family media plan to help you balance media and tech (theirs and yours) with all of the other things that are important to you. This isn't just for them; it's for you, too. Schedule in downtime, chores, homework, outdoor fun, reading, meals, etc. And then figure out how much extra is available for TV shows, games, apps and other media activities. Don't worry about counting up daily screen time minutes -- just aim for a balance throughout the week. Try to carve out times and locations that are "screen-free zones." Hold yourself to them. Kids learn more from what we do than what we say, so make sure you're role-modeling the right habits.

VIRTUAL VICTMIZATION

Of course, virtual reality is not reality, but differentiating between what is seen in real life and the images seen on screens, is very difficult. Internet video may be more realistic to youngsters than actually being there! Experiencing the 3 dimensional graphic details of a new video system can mesmerize youngsters and convince even the best of us. Through screens, today, come visual images of such clarity that our perceptions of the world, through the screen, often become our reality. Our neurological pathways deliver the message bringing us to the point that our virtual experience may register as "actual experience" within our brains. The effect of possible confusion for kids, who interact with their physical and virtual worlds in an almost seamless manner, is a popular area of media research.

One of my primary concerns is that young, impressionable people can actually become victimized by things they have witnessed and "experienced" on film and video. This virtual victimization of our post-millennials is further reinforced by their tremendous consumption of media. Psychologists used to believe that one had to directly experience - or personally witness - a traumatic event in order to be severely affected by it. It was assumed that only those individuals *physically present* or *actually there*, could become casualties of violence, abuse or terror. But the Internet and television have changed all that, providing imagery and close-up experiences of such clarity and potency that perceptions of events via screens have become reality for many.

A virtual experience, particularly after being viewed repetitively, can, actually hijack the brain into registering screen images as reality. The virtual victimization of those who watched the events of 9/11 unfold on TV screens from the safety of their homes, experienced similar emotional distress to those who were physically proximate to the horrific event. The flick of a TV-switch created virtual victims of viewers everywhere, as they "experienced" the horror of the World Trade Towers crumbling.

It's important to understand that repeated on-air images can become integrated into the first-hand witnessing of events and, ultimately, the real life memories of media consumers. Large numbers of children across the country and the world experienced trauma on 9/11 and were severely affected by the occurrence, even though they were far from the scene. Now, years later, many people report that even mentions of 9/11 will trigger anxiety and stress. Both adult and child virtual victims still, today, experience flashbacks, reoccurring thoughts and anxiety that interferes with the ability to focus and with sleep.

Protecting children in a complex media environment is confounding, as screen-based trauma often occurs suddenly and unexpectedly. In addition, repetitive exposure of powerful images – be they glorious or disturbing – do not just "go away" when the TV is turned off or the tablet put away. Some children will experience trauma watching an upsetting news story, yet bury those thoughts and images. This does not mean, of course, that the child is not affected, or won't experience future flashbacks or nightmares. Months or even years later, these same images may disturb that same iGen individual in a totally unrelated context. With many images ruminating in the brain, it is impossible to predict which recollections and memories could act as emotional triggers in the future.

When evaluating the exposure of youngsters to a wide range of visual subject matter on the web, cognitive development and age are critical factors in assessing risk. Since young children have a greater vulnerability to experiencing trauma from witnessing frightening events than do adults, even a glimpse of a highly disturbing occurrence can be extremely distressing to process. Media's powerful images do not go unnoticed by kids, and they are rarely completely forgotten.

Events that are visually reported in the news media can cause or trigger a frightful memory. Disasters such as floods, school shootings, car crashes or fires can cause extreme stress and anticipatory anxiety. Traumatizing events, including the reporting of a sexual assault or other violent crime, may particularly resonate and register within a child's memory. Often, this leads to confusion about which events children have experienced and which they might have seen on the news. For some youngsters, repeated media images of a bombing, kidnapping or an earthquake may be so powerful and intense that they cannot differentiate the actual catastrophe from the video. Sounds add to their perceptions, memories and responses.

Following any kind of trauma, even virtual trauma, children may initially show agitated or confused behavior. They also may show intense fear, helplessness and anger. Sometimes, digital natives will deaden their emotions and dissociate, revealing nothing but a numb response whenever the traumatic event is mentioned. iGen consumers of media are particularly vulnerable to trauma reactions and anxiety disorders. Parents should be careful to limit their own viewing of news in the home and focus their conversations about catastrophic events to discussions of individuals, like first responders, who have demonstrated bravery or compassion. Sadly, news stories which involve young children in horrific situations create additional stress and anxiety.

There is such a wide range of reactions to traumatic events that it is impossible to predict the impact upon any specific individual. One child's response to a loud noise or the brush of wind can trigger a fear reaction, a desire to fight or an urge to flee. For another child, the only physical reaction to a stimuli perceived as threatening is a subtle elevation in heart rate.

Chances are if your home has a TV, your post-millennial child is already a virtual victim. In the same way that survivors of the Holocaust and combat veterans experienced post-traumatic stress disorder (PTSD) after their horrific experiences, kids' memories of what they have seen on television or the Internet, may produce effects that are anything but virtual. Children suffering from PTSD may show signs of their condition in their play and behavior. For example, there may be more pretend shooting after experiencing the TV reporting of a school shooting or even a more generalized series of angry and aggressive behaviors.

Youngsters respond to visuals and film clips, regardless if the event comes, or does not come, to fruition. The prediction of hurricanes and disasters can cause large-scale emotional trauma for post-millennials. This is true even of documentary footage where there is no actual, predicted disaster. Importantly, if iGen kids sense their parents have little or no control over world events or weather, it increases their anxiety and that anxiety can escalate around stress.

Children worry about what terrible things might occur. But, in the case of news - be it a school shooting or a terrorist attack, it is something that did, actually, happen. Worst case scenario is a traumatic event that happened to a close family member or a same-age child in a familiar safe setting; a home fire, assault at a day care center. The obvious and most surreal response is if this could happen to a child *like* me, will it happen to me?

For those of us who are old enough to remember standing behind the door to "hide" from scary scenes in TV movies -- phones and tablets have also changed all that. Avoiding unrelenting media images is not an easy option. In a simpler time, parents would wait until the children were asleep and turn on the 11 o'clock news. Not anymore.

Media is ubiquitous, intense and seductive. Alerts and disturbing footage from natural disasters and war zones appear everywhere, including on grandma's Apple watch. Video screens – in elevators, at the gas station and in the supermarket enable consumers to experience the effect of being directly at a crime scene or accident. "Newsproofing" a young child's environment is more difficult, but probably, more necessary today than ever before. Of course, parenting would be a whole lot easier, if we could edit news footage and bleep out all news alerts before kids started asking us "what happened?" In a competitive media environment with late-breaking alerts and updates from the scenes of accidents and disasters, the news landscape can be distressing and scary. "If it bleeds it leads," the essential cable and Internet news marketing strategy, could make even the staunchest supporters of the First Amendment yearn for more editing of news when kids are nearby.

In addition, much of kids' entertainment and news viewing and listening today is done in isolation. Individual and mobile screens have taken us away from family discussions around the kitchen table. For digital natives, most news gathering is a solo activity and watching and reflecting upon current events has circumvented the parental oversight it requires. Anyone who has witnessed a child's nightmare based on a newscast knows that even a snippet of a story could, in a moment, have a powerful impact on that child. Back in the day, the kids went to bed before the news came on, and parents could prevent the upsetting content from greater family exposure.

There has, of course, always been disturbing media images viewed inadvertently or even accidentally by children. But, these incidences were fewer and, for the most part, less punishing than anything a youngster might experience today. Exposure to news reports and video can alter and shape a child's sense of reality. We know that young people are strongly influenced by the images they see. News reports can resonate and can fill their world view with anxiety and apprehension.

The realism of news, can be overwhelming for children as it conveys an anticipatory anxiety about what awaits. Following a major news report, ongoing post-trauma concerns about dying, the death of family members at an early age and the world as a scary and unsafe place, can preoccupy suggestible children for months. Panic attacks, phobias and nightmares may follow.

It is important that parents continuously model calm and self-control. Children, of course, are emotionally vulnerable and need reassurance and support. They need to know they are safe and there are trustworthy people they can rely on.

It's been said that the tone and presentation of reports on a news event will also play a distinct role in how the message is received. The messenger, a dispassionate reporter, may utter facts in a complete monotone in order to be accurate and appear unemotional. Unfortunately, this matter-of-fact delivery may contribute additional lack of empathy to the desensitization of young viewers, unrelated to the real suffering and violence that they see on their screens.

NOTE TO PARENTS ABOUT VIRTUAL TRAUMA: We know how traumatizing media images of a natural disaster like a hurricane or earthquake can be, even when viewed inadvertently by a young child. The National Association of School Psychologists (NASP) (https://www.nasponline.org), has produced excellent materials to help youngsters cope with difficult images following exposure to a trauma, disaster or violent attack seen on the news.

WHO'S WATCHING WHAT OUR KIDS ARE WATCHING?

When it comes to the oversight of media content for kids and families, including news, there is very little scrutiny by companies that create and distribute this content. A significant change in the media industry has been the disappearance of any mediator or protective shield in the supervision of kids' exposure to digital content and entertainment. Until the explosion of programming on numerous platforms other than television, parents could have relied on tools such as v-chips, blocking devices, rating systems and a "third eye", like the Standards and Practices departments of TV networks, to review programming for appropriateness for young audiences. Although there are occasional monitors on large Internet forums and clearance staff at large commercial entities, there is little content oversight, editing or censorship for protection of the child audience in the today's entertainment realm.

Government organizations like the Federal Communications Commission (FCC) and industry groups like the Motion Picture Association of America (MPAA), the Entertainment Software Rating Board (ESRB) and the Children's Advertising Review Unit (CARU) of the Council of Better Business Bureaus, provide guidelines and hotlines to help parents monitor and limit kids' access to unsuitable or harmful entertainment, content and advertising. However, even with these watchdog groups monitoring, children's direct access to the Internet on open devises has weakened the parent advocacy safety net. Kids' direct access to the source - the Internet - has, obviously, diminished the strength of any oversight process.

There is also no cop on the Internet beat to make sure the information that our children access is truthful and accurate. Since the Internet is anonymous and public, one doesn't need press credentials or a fact-checker to create or promote the stories or substantiate the authenticity of things you want to sell on the web. Photos of newsworthy events distributed on Snapchat and other social media services are often altered or arranged out of context, to achieve a specific effect. Instagram and Facebook users regularly curate and photo-shop their posts. On-line sources, like Wikipedia, admit an inability to legally verify any information, as anyone can hack, edit and add misinformation.

Adolescents and teens may not be skeptical of headlines, even when they appear to be over-the-top and totally fabricated. They may also be fooled by the names of URL's that are very close to the URL for a legitimate site. Numerous tricks are used to entice viewers and readers to bogus sites that look almost identical to authentic, registered websites. This is confusing to all, but particularly unfair to digital natives who have yet to develop the subtle ability to read between the blurs in the lines.

Improved technology has undoubtedly energized the fake news process, with blue screens and photo-shopping altering what's supposed to be reality and diminishing our ability to differentiate between what is real and what is not. Fake news is comprised of made-up stories, partial truths, exaggerations and hoaxes. With similar typefaces and logos, fake news articles look remarkably like those we know to be credible and can fool even the most sophisticated adults. Of course, GenZ kids can be easily manipulated by fake news because of their inexperience and the product's slick presentation.

At first, many news stories may seem to be legitimate. However, these stories might contain inaccuracies that are not immediately apparent. Importantly, they can serve to communicate a specific point of view or have an agenda that either supports or hurts a group or individual. The confusion doesn't stop with multiple delivery systems streaming totally fictitious news or misleading content. Although fake news is not a new phenomenon, it has become increasingly difficult to distinguish actual news from fictitious reporting, and that goes for kids and adults, alike. Parents are more concerned than ever that their kids will be easily influenced, taken advantage of and persuaded to act against their better judgement by what they hear and read on social media.

NOTE TO PARENTS CONCERNED ABOUT THE DEVELOPMENT OF THEIR CHILD'S CRITICAL THINKING SKILLS: We want our post-millennials to be curious and trusting. We also want them to be smart and skeptical consumers of information and question the reliability, truthfulness and accuracy of what they hear and see on the web.

SEXUALIZATION

Growing up, young girls see continuous aspirational images of grown women receiving positive reinforcement for their sexuality. Hard to imagine that girls as young as three, may already be skilled at striking sexy poses, batting their eyelashes and receiving favorable adult attention for it. At the same time, they may also receive feedback that their other qualities and talents don't get half of the interest or regard that acting sexy delivers.

While watching pre-school fashionistas wearing off-the-shoulder outfits copied from the wardrobes of Britney and the Kardashians, it's not hard to see the impact and potency of sexualization in our culture. When a young girl perceives her value as a person is derived almost exclusively from her sex appeal, a red flag should be raised and parents *should* be worried. Although there is concern among the medical, faith-based and educational communities regarding sexualization trends in current-day society, girls and women today still report that much of their self-esteem is a result of positive comments about their looks and appeal. Children's clothing manufacturers who target tweens argue that it is the parents who purchase provocative bare midriff and micro mini outfits for their daughters. Although parents may say they disapprove of these sexualized and age-inappropriate fashions, their clothing dollars are flowing.

Attitudes around body image, especially when presented early in life, are impactful. Although boys are affected as well, issues related to physique and self-esteem are of particular influence in the self-actualization process of young women. Negative feedback regarding young girls' physical appearance may lay the groundwork for lifelong struggles with depression and eating disorders. And, even if the overt feedback isn't negative, a young woman's self-evaluation and self-scorn can result in devastating psychological consequences.

I used to assume that girls' positive self-worth would improve in proportion to growth in the numbers of successful, professional female role models they knew and interacted with. An increase in the number of women with college and graduate degrees, professional credentials and workplace successes could provide helpful models and real life experiences for young women to emulate. However, studies conducted over the last three decades consistently show little movement, if any, in measurements of girls' self-esteem. Young women still report that academic achievement and other talents do not get the social reinforcement or the positive recognition they deserve. With obsessive glimpses in the mirror and habitual monitoring of one's looks, girls begin to see themselves through the eyes of others and are influenced to adopt a third-party perspective known as "self-objectification."

We live in a hyper-sexualized culture. On-line posts and the format of social media web ratings, unfortunately, only strengthen the GenZ perception of girls as sexual objects. And, after spending numerous hours on the Internet, many female digital natives have come to see themselves in the same objectified way. Some may argue that families, social communities, educational institutions and the Internet all share in the responsibility of raising confident girls. However, we are still left with a large group of adolescent and teen girls believing that, to a large extent, popularity and success are completely determined by appearance.

As a direct result of some post-millennials' total preoccupation with their looks, there are simply fewer moments in the day for other thoughts or activities of any kind. Adolescent girls regularly report concentration problems because of hunger issues and the fact that they spend so much of their time contemplating being pretty enough, sexy enough and popular enough. We know that when girls are overly focused on their physical appearance, they become distracted from other important socialization activities, academic pursuits and sports. According to the American Psychological Association's Task Force on the Sexualization of Girls, sexualization occurs when an individual's value as a person comes, exclusively, from her sexual appeal or behavior, to the exclusion of almost everything else about her. This is echoed by educators and medical professionals, including child therapists who claim that the obsessive need to be thin and sexy is the elephant in the room when young women discuss their depressive disorders.

As screens provide greater access to programming and advertising featuring idealized adult female images, young girls are introduced to those images with little, if any, exposure to what *real* women's bodies look like. The ten-year-old who wanted to look sexy and dress like Britney may now be a mother, herself and reading this book. But, the effects of the insidious sexualization process may still influence her feelings about her own competence and self-worth.

The "adultification" process, which gives favorable feedback to girls who look and act older, as well as highly sexualized, is another area of concern in this process. Perhaps nothing better illustrates the adultification and sexualization of young girls than child beauty pageants. Before our eyes, little girls morph into sexy beauty queens with heavy makeup and super-model hairstyles and clothing. TV programs like *Toddlers and Tiaras* have explored these pageants and have shown young contestants who are made-up to look like little adults, often pushed into the limelight by competitive mothers. Many of these mothers were, themselves, brought up on this highly sexualized programming and may also have been influenced by stereotyped media representations of women.

Like other competitive pursuits, youngsters are particularly vulnerable to anxieties when they are confronted with extreme standards for success or rejection. Cultivating this idealized image of women and their physical attributes sets an unreasonable and unhealthy bar for many girls. Looks-oriented beauty contests, showing young kids costumed with perfectionistic detail and attention to their sexuality further reinforces these attributes and stereotypes.

The "Naughty-Sexy-Schoolgirl" caricature, another idealized image, has captured the imagination of many social media users. This Lolita-type schoolgirl demonstrates "youthification," a complimentary trend in sexualized media images and music videos. Christina Aguilera's original adult vixen, lollipop in hand and shirt unbuttoned to reveal cleavage, illustrates an increasingly common depiction of mature women attempting to be little girls -- and little girls, pretending to be grown-up women trying to gain the attention of men. This message is concerning and complex for kids and their parents to understand. Some of these same motivations may also appeal to individuals seeking out kiddie porn.

There are numerous cognitive and emotional consequences as well as mental health risks associated with the sexualization process. Constant self-objectification very often leads to low self-esteem as well as an array of body and identity issues. The compelling need to be thin has resulted in the median age for the onset of eating disorders to be just twelve- years-old. The

National Eating Disorders Association concludes that in the U.S. alone, twenty million women will suffer from symptoms of anorexia nervosa, bulimia or binge eating sometime during their lives.

Anorexia nervosa, the disorder of excessive food restriction, plays havoc on the body and the central nervous system. As girls struggle to maintain as thin a physique as possible, controlling their eating by severely curbing food intake also deprives their organs of essential nutrients. Ultimately, this starvation-diet behavior can result in heart failure, muscle loss and kidney and liver shutdown. Anorexia nervosa doesn't just result in weight loss; it has an alarming 20% mortality rate. Still, the message for young women through media and throughout their lives is to be thin at all costs.

Sexualization and self-objectification undermine the self-confidence and happiness that young women deserve. As little girls grow up, they may embrace expectations including becoming a model, a princess or a ballerina. These projections begin as normal and appropriate role playing activities, but for some children - including boys - childhood images of adulthood can become obsessions that are physically inappropriate and difficult to manage. Along with the pressure to stay thin, the craving to be recognized for youthful beauty and sexual appeal can promote insecurity, extreme self-consciousness and a range of psychological problems.

NOTE TO PARENTS WHO ARE WORRIED ABOUT THE OVER-SEXUALIZATION OF THEIR DAUGHTERS: The sexualization of our society convinces young women that in order to secure love and attention from the opposite sex, you must be thinner and sexier than you already are. Regrettably, young girls hear this message loud and clear.

The Healthy Teen Project, (healthyteenproject.com) is a therapeutic program for the treatment of eating disorders. Their informational website helps parents understand the early warning signs of Anorexia, Bulimia and Binge Eating Disorders.

The Healthy Teen Project's Warning signs of Anorexia, Bulimia and Binge Eating Disorders:

http://www.healthyteenproject.com

"Teenagers with anorexia may take extreme measures to avoid eating and control the quantity and quality of the foods they do eat.

Signs of Anorexia may include:

- A distorted view of one's body weight, size or shape; sees self as too fat, even when very underweight
- Hiding or discarding food
- Obsessively counting calories and/or grams of fat in the diet
- Denial of feelings of hunger
- Developing rituals around preparing food and eating
- Compulsive or excessive exercise
- Social withdrawal
- Pronounced emotional changes, such as irritability, depression and anxiety

Physical signs of anorexia include rapid or excessive weight loss; feeling cold, tired and weak; thinning hair; absence of menstrual cycles in females; and dizziness or fainting.

Teenagers with anorexia often restrict not only food, but relationships, social activities and pleasurable experiences.

Bulimia:

Teenagers with bulimia nervosa typically 'binge and purge' by engaging in uncontrollable episodes of overeating (bingeing) usually followed by compensatory behavior such as: purging through vomiting, use of laxatives, enemas, fasting, or excessive exercise. Eating binges may occur as often as several times a day but are most common in the evening and night hours.

Teenagers with bulimia often go unnoticed due to the ability to maintain a normal body weight.

Signs of bulimia may include:

Eating unusually large amounts of food with no apparent change in weight

- Hiding food or discarded food containers and wrappers
- Excessive exercise or fasting
- Peculiar eating habits or rituals
- Frequent trips to the bathroom after meals
- Inappropriate use of laxatives, diuretics, or other cathartics
- Overachieving and impulsive behaviors
- Frequently clogged showers or toilets

Physical signs of bulimia include discolored teeth, odor on the breath, stomach pain, calluses/scarring on the hands caused by self-inducing vomiting, irregular or absent menstrual periods, and weakness or fatigue.

Teenagers with bulimia often have a preoccupation with body weight and shape, as well as a distorted body image. The clinical diagnosis commonly defines a teenager as having bulimia if they binge and purge on average once a week for at least three consecutive months.

Binge Eating Disorders:

Binge eating disorder is characterized by a sense of uncontrollable excessive eating, followed by feelings of shame and guilt. Unlike those with bulimia, however, teenagers with binge eating disorders typically do not compensate for their binges.

Teenagers with binge eating disorder are typically overweight.

They may feel like they have no control over their behavior and eat in secret when they are not hungry.

<u>Signs of Binge Eating Disorder might include:</u>

- Eating unusually large amounts of food in a distinct period of time (within 2 hours)
- Eating rapidly
- Hiding food or discarded food containers and wrappers
- Eating in secret because of feeling embarrassed by how much they are eating
- Eating when stressed or when feeling uncertain how to cope
- Feeling that they are unable to control how much they eat and disgusted with themselves afterwards
- Experimentation with different diets"

WHAT MAKES TEENS TICK AND CLICK?

Teens may have outgrown their parents in height already, but they are by no means, neurologically, fully formed. It's during the teen years that the executive functions of the brain increase in development and become refined. These processes include the ability to utilize past experiences to solve current problems and the capability to organize and prioritize tasks. Mastery of these functions are critical for the development of a risk-adverse adult "braking" system where one can stop and review data before acting and then project connections between behavior and long-term consequences.

There is clear evidence that teens are prone to risk-taking behaviors and that there is a biochemical basis underlying this conduct. Not only do 12 to 20-year-olds often have difficulty controlling their impulses in the moment, but their strong sense of immortality makes it tough for them to see the connections between their actions today and consequences, tomorrow. This carefree behavior and skewed perception of invincibility reinforces risk taking, both on and off the Internet. Impulsivity and risk-taking are typical characteristics of teens, who may often be unaware of the potential dangers they face. As these digital natives try to develop risk-adverse behavioral controls, the natural presence of the chemical, Dopamine in the brain may, actually, undermine some of their ability to do so.

Dopamine is a naturally produced neurotransmitter in the brain that affects mood, sleep, memory and the ability to focus. Like an internal messenger responsible for sending notifications directly from the central nervous system to the brain, Dopamine allows information to be passed from one neuron to another, helping to seek out pleasurable, desirable and rewarding activities. In particular, Dopamine kicks in to reward and keep the wanted behaviors returning to the same place that we know has already brought pleasure.

Guided by tiny Dopamine "pings" or shocks to the brain, the result is a heightened awareness and involvement in risk-oriented activities. These are the same Dopamine- producing nerve cells that naturally activate the reward circuitry of the brain and support other motivations as well. This is also called the winning response and a high, successful feeling. For runners, this is the kick of "being in the zone".

Considered the natural chemical connection to success and a basic building block of learning, Dopamine is supported by a response cocktail comprised of Serotonin and Oxytocin along with other endorphins and hormones. These neurotransmitters are responsible for the powerful bond between the causes and effects of behavior reinforcement. It's the chemistry of Oprah's "Aha" moment and the conditioned response of achievement. This can also be felt after an e-bay sale or by throwing a virtual baseball on the Wii which connects the on-line user to the sensation of victory. Neurologists have found that teens have higher levels of Dopamine and lower sensitivity to it, than do younger kids or older people. They may understand dangers and risks, intellectually, but emotionally, still feel invincible. It's the ping of perseverance and motivation needed to stay in the groove. Internet usage utilizes this same process of increasing personal on-line interaction and participation. In addition to the chemical basis for behavior, we now know genes and

DR. HELEN BOEHM

other family traits also influence impulsivity and risk-taking behaviors.

Still, when parents are trying to make sense of their adolescent or teenaged children, psychologists always lead them back to the developing brain. High school students may have adequate social and academic skills, but may also feel indestructible and act recklessly. It is unnerving to see kids in JV basketball behaving like 4-year-old wanna-be-Power Rangers, with no "off" switch on their power grid.

The more we learn more about the developing brain, the better we are able to understand its role in the complex activities of emotional self-regulation and the ability to avoid risk. Parents often complain that their kids "get stuck" and don't have the flexibility to explore a range of solutions to problems. What they are actually describing, is a neurological reality of the teen years. If these post-millennials are inflexible and stubborn, it's because their brains are still in the process of developing fluidity in their thinking. Developmentally, they are in simultaneous overdrive, trying to balance their impulses with an increasing knowledge base of what is right and wrong.

"We lived on farms. We lived in cities. Now we live on the internet," were words spoken by Justin Timberlake as he played the social media entrepreneur, Sean Parker, in Aaron Sorkin's film, *The Social Network*. Post-millennials use their on-line lives to explore a world that opens with ease as they conduct video chats and play interactive games. They may spend their nights lying in wait for a "ping," so they can read what someone has said to them, or about them. They check out fashions and fantasy sports between texting, tweeting, creating and curating their own digital identities.

Parents have voiced concern about inconsistencies between their teen's virtual/social representation on the Internet and their actual - off-line - identities. And, to add to any identity confusion, if a digital native's on-line persona doesn't quite correspond to the physical girl or guy they imagine themselves to be, they can alter, delete or photo-shop their image until they achieve a virtual persona that is their best, authentic self. Web lives may be complex and multifaceted, but rarely are they completely accurate.

Parents must also prepare for numerous lies, poisonous ideas and terrible images that their kids will be exposed to on the web. We may find iGen teens listening to irresponsible opinions or even affected by anti-social or violent material. Our kids may involuntarily encounter videos glamourizing hatred or see images of illegal drug use. An awareness of the unruly landscape of the World Wide Web will be necessary if you are to assist and prepare kids for the content they may encounter on-line. We know how difficult many of these images are to process, but we haven't even scratched the surface in understanding the cumulative impact of exposure to hate and horror over a long period of time. It is important that parents are there to mediate many of the ideas and images their kids will be seeing, hearing or even experiencing on-line. We probably cannot prevent net exposure all together, but we can mitigate some of its impact and influence.

Post-millennials have particular difficulties walking away from social media and restraining their time on the net. For these youngsters, most of their non-school and non-sleeping hours are spent either on the net or playing video games. Digital natives check their social media accounts multiple times per hour to find out what others are saying about them and who is challenging their relationships, looks or popularity. They are focused on relationship status, who is "in" and who is not. Since the concern among youngsters regarding their status is so profound, a large number of teens follow the on-line accounts of their frenemies as well as their friends. Using the net is easy, but the bumps experienced during the teen years can be difficult going.

As today's tech-savvy youngsters interact with on-line information, they seem to instinctively utilize the highly evolutionary skill of cutting through the clutter. The process consists of sorting, linking, mining, and drilling down to discover, compile and combine content. Post-millennials deal with large amounts of data, information and images. They intuitively unravel net obstacles and resolve technical glitches with lightning speed, but they are often unable to deconstruct what they did or explain how they did it. Kids have access to it all as the web takes its place as the world's largest classroom.

The same awesome high-tech formulas that guide you through traffic using the fastest route, can deliver content to your personal e-mail account, based upon your specific interests, word searches, fantasies and movies rented. Easy access to all content on the net - including sexually oriented material - is a reality that is now never more than a click away. Of course, GenZ teens have been exposed to X-rated images and early sexual experimentation through numerous media and life-style influences. There are films, cable television shows, sexy anime and porn magazines. But, the particular contribution of Internet-delivered sexual information is, undeniably, the most formidable.

We know that young people strive to be as sexually experienced as they believe their peers to be, and the "everybody's doing it" message certainly amplifies our GenZ member's personal enthusiasm for keeping up with the group. The confirmation that cool kids "do it" creates an implied permission across social media that it's ok to do a number of things, including having sex because (almost) everyone else is.

HOW DIGITAL MODELS
SPREAD... CONTAGION

The psychological construct of contagion describes the spread of an emotion or behavior. In the same way that a YouTube video goes viral or a pebble creates ripples after being tossed into a pond, contagion expands like "jumping on a bandwagon" into shaping, modeling and influencing the most impressionable in its path. Kids are particularly vulnerable to the contagion that pulls them to the Internet and influences both their thoughts and actions.

Styles and fashion trends, including wardrobes for model-thin girls, spread quickly through the world-wide web. But, along with influencing how kids should *look* comes the very tricky inducement regarding how they should *act*. The spread of a trend can be as innocuous as a new sneaker fad or as terrible as the contagion effect of copy-cat behavior following a teen suicide. In the case of a death by suicide, just the reporting of a young person's demise on the news can be a powerful stimulus for both suicide ideation and attempts by other youngsters. The contagion of an idea especially attracts the emotionally fragile and vulnerable iGen child and readily connects with their impulsivity.

Enter Internet and social media contagion, a powerful spread of information, ideas and images forwarded along to the people you know or may want to know, as well as those you wish to follow and "be like". Contagion expands from person to person, constantly influencing and being influenced by the attitudes of others. For most individuals, particularly the GenZ demographic, there is a social media imperative to model people, ideas and behaviors that are aspirational and popular. In order to stay motivated to participate, young people rush to develop followers, demonstrate being liked and popular and, ultimately, establishing their own social currency. Sometimes, it is the secret interaction between a teen and her cell phone as she obsessively reviews photos of too-thin fashion models and chides herself with negative comparisons. At other times, it involves jumping on the bandwagon and being influenced by the powerful images and commanding ideas that resonate on screens.

The spread, or contagion, of ideas through social media runs quickly and deeply. One terrible, but powerful example of this effect is the widespread problem of teen self-harm and suicide. It is known, for example, that the reporting of the details as to how a suicide was achieved is extremely dangerous and can click very strongly in the mind of an impressionable young person. Within seconds, a resolution to a problem is revealed and, along with it, a road map for behavior with specific instructions.

Social media's role in both encouraging and discouraging vulnerable individuals to perform certain behaviors is complex. Although media can be a positive force for raising awareness and providing safety information and resources, its influence on suicidality and self-harming behavior among young people raises genuine concerns. News, social media, the net and digital entertainment may share in the responsibility of offering increased risk of media contagion, by the very act of focusing attention on a subject and presenting a narrative that suicide was used as a means of solving a problem. Many experts agree that even the simple description or announcement of a suicide may, unintentionally, contaminate a young individual and result in conveying a legitimacy of such an act.

Since more digital natives die from suicide than homicide and the rate of suicide among adolescents and teens continues to rise, it's important to view the Internet and social media as both parts of the solution as well as the problem. Death by suicide has risen among teens, some of whom may have been influenced by things they saw and learned on the Internet. But social media can also be a valuable support system and potential safety net for youngsters at risk. There are extensive social media programs which assist post-millennials to talk about their feelings with parents and friends and encourage them to connect with organizations, hotlines and counseling services. Establishing a global outreach and support mechanism for communication, interventions and lifesaving services around the world is technology fulfilling its best potential.

Readers of this book may have also viewed the recent popular Netflix TV series, "13 Reasons Why," which brought the crisis of teen suicide into classrooms and living rooms. Although it helped to raise a positive national conversation on the subject of teen depression and suicide, I had several concerns about the program that I would like to share with parents:

Firstly, I was concerned about the inclusion of the instructional aspects of the suicide act within the program. Showing the details of the young woman taking her own life, even for reference, provided a "how-to" roadmap for young, vulnerable viewers. In addition, the program offered unnecessary specificity for the reasons leading to the suicide, suggesting a legitimacy of the technique under certain conditions. At the conclusion of the series, a measurement of Internet searches for things like "suicide hotline," "suicide prevention" and "teen suicide" demonstrated the program's positive sharing of important resources. However, parents should be aware that there were equally large numbers of searches for "how to commit suicide" and "how to kill yourself."

In the Snapchat and Twitter world, it is important not to trigger certain thoughts and behaviors by sensationalizing or romanticizing a death by suicide. In particular, excessive details about how an act of suicide was committed and possible reasons, like, "My boyfriend broke up with me," or "My selfie went viral," should always be avoided. Also of grave concern to parents are the unmonitored chat rooms where discussions of suicide and individual postings may, inexplicably, encourage an ambivalent person to move forward with taking their own life. Those types of sites and virtual experiences should be off limits to all young people.

When a tragedy, such as the suicide of a well-known young individual or cool celebrity occurs, the impact on digital natives is particularly profound. News via social media has an enormous influence on our culture, as the combination of the most powerful act one can commit is coupled with the most powerful tool to relay one's story. The unfortunate negative effects of such occurrences are devastating to parents, families and communities.

NOTE TO PARENTS WHO ARE CONCERNED ABOUT SUICIDE IDEATION AND THE COPY-CAT PHENOMENON: There are many excellent resources in the area of youth suicide available on the Internet. Numerous educational and awareness programs can equip young people, youth workers and parents with tools and resources for identifying and assisting kids at risk.

Along with prevention affiliates and partners, the Jason Foundation (JFI) (JASONFOUNDATION.org) provides materials and seminars on the "silent epidemic" of youth suicide. The foundation is particularly concerned about young people who are have feelings of hopelessness and are preoccupied with thoughts about death and suicide. JFI also suggests that parents are aware of their children's unusual behaviors and other risk factors, such as low self-esteem, learning challenges and childhood trauma that could, possibly, elevate suicidal ideation.

SOCIAL/ UNSOCIAL MEDIA

Social networks are as old as time, it's just now they're digital and include more people than can fit around a dining room table. Our kids are spending much of their day in front of a screen, shaping and sharpening their digital ID's and creating their unique public personalities. GenZ's preferred on-line social networks include Vine, Instagram and Twitter and are, essentially, digital extensions of their off-line lives. Given the amount of time dedicated to chronicling their every move and meal, teens' "Sarahahing," tweeting and snapping have become more of a lifestyle than simply a means of staying in touch with social friends.

Being "liked" and "followed" in social media have become the currency of the post-millennial crowd. Young people spend a great deal of thought and time curating their best selves, photo-shopping their pimples away and even editing their photos to appear to be more popular than they actually are IRL (in real life). It's no surprise that members of this over-sharing generation are hooked on gaining visibility and popularity. The net's international reach to teens in on-line virtual communities everywhere is expansive. Through sharing on sites and apps like Facebook, Instagram, WhatsApp, Kik, Tumblr, Flickr, Houseparty and Twitter, young people continuously reinvent themselves and market their latest and best versions. After spending far more effort in the creation of a virtual life than in living an actual one, parents may think their post-millennial teens would be worn out by the social media process. But, it seems to be never ending!

Parents are concerned that social media may cause excessive anxiety and an excessive need for constant reassurance and social validation. Certainly, wanting to be liked and popular is not a new trend for adolescents and teens. However, this level of obsessive checking, posting and sharing on social networks is troubling. The current extreme demand for approval and validation can turn a friendly skype session into a nerve-racking event. The craving for social assurance and constant approval is associated with excessive use of social media, but this need is not, necessarily, caused by social media, itself.

Young users of on-line social media often admit to feeling drained and depressed after several hours of non-stop sharing. Still, they seem to persevere and continue their interaction and on-line presence. The compulsive use of social media to stay "liked" and connected may, sometimes, end with feelings of even greater isolation and loneliness. These feelings may be alleviated by friendly affirmations found on the net, occasional messages from friends or acquaintances, or even a look through amusing Emoji's.

GenZ teens are constantly measuring their own on-line popularity and friendships by collecting approvals from followers for everything from their sports accomplishments to their hair color. Even while receiving wide exposure, good feedback and lots of "likes," the process of sharing and receiving criticism on social media can contribute to emotional overload. One must be extremely careful about posting, not leaving tracks and not hurting the feelings of others. And, to add to levels of anxiety, young social media users are often distressed about the negative effects of FOMO (Fear of Missing Out) when they see evidence of gatherings or parties to which they were not invited.

The need for continuous reinforcement and recognition can become so disruptive that it interferes with one's physical emotional functioning. Feeling left out and worrying about acceptance by peers takes a major toll on all levels of confidence and self-esteem. This may also be compounded by continuous "friending" and "unfriending" by both virtual and real-life contacts. Finally, sleep deprivation exacerbates this anxiety, as youngsters bring their iPhones into bed in anticipation of reading posts that might be for or about them during the night. Now, sleeplessness combined with a constant state of web arousal and worry has limited our digital natives' capacity for relaxation, emotional self-regulation and sleep.

GenZ members move seamlessly between their on- and off-line lives. But, on social media, their basic impulsivity may cause them to reveal more information than they should. Teens may appear confident in revealing details about themselves on the Internet that they would never think of telling others IRL (in real life). Using social media can also be risky for youngsters who tend to "over share" and don't fully understand that their lack of discretion can have serious negative implications moving forward. Would you ever trust a social confessional app called Whisper that lets users share their feelings, anonymously, to remain … anonymous?

Of course, social media participation also provides some awesome opportunities for socialization, learning and communication. Connecting with family and friends, making new friends, sharing pictures and exchanging ideas are fun and beneficial activities to be encouraged. Social media can also build community for Post-Millennials, who have the distinction of being the first generation to have their own births announced on Facebook!

During the past few years, major influencers from politicians to professors and entertainers are utilizing social network technologies to tweet and to text and reach out to as many people as possible. Various social networks offer post-millennials a deeper understanding of themselves and their cultures and an extension of their world view. Interacting with people from all over the world builds tolerance, interest in languages and culture and increased discourse about personal and global issues. Technology has probably made post-millennials from around the world more tolerant and more open to new ideas than members of all generations that preceded them.

Parents, however, are concerned about the amount of time kids are on social media and most mental health professionals disapprove of both the quality and quantity of time young people spend on these websites. Studies confirm that emotionally fragile adolescents and teens, in the process of discovering who they are and their own identities, would probably benefit from less time and exposure to social networks. Active users, who are on-line making social connections, report more favorable use of their time than passive users, who hang around these sites watching others and gaining information. Passive users also claim to have more negative and envious feelings when reading the posts and boasts of others.

Very young kids should not play in a public park by themselves and they shouldn't be on social media by themselves, either. Even when parents are engaged and supervising their children, many websites surreptitiously provide user information to marketers, data aggregators and tracking companies. This is why one of the few federal regulations governing the Internet in the U.S. is the Children's Online Privacy Protection Act (COPPA). This act, implemented by the Federal Trade Commission (FTC), imposes compliance obligations on websites that collect personal information from and about children under thirteen without parental permission. Fortunately, there are many age-appropriate social media sites that are both COPPA compliant and respect kids' privacy. These safe sites for kids include PlayKids Talk - Kids-Safe Messenger, for 7-8 year-olds,

Kuddle, PLAYMessenger: Child Safe Chat and iTwixie, for 8-9 year-olds, and Franktown Rock, Kidzworld and Sweety High, for 10-12 year olds. However, even careful parents may, unknowingly, contribute private information about their kids to advertisers and marketers at any time, through on-line transactions, on pay pal or GPS trackers.

Adults, who have spent decades in familiar Internet patterns like eBay and school reunion websites, are often surprised to find themselves pulled into social media as a daily form of interaction. Like their kids, many adults began social media habits by contacting old friends and making new ones. Now, exposed to a multitude of new opportunities, infinite communities and relationships, parents have joined their kids on the net. All of this being reminiscent of broadcast television's entertainment programming for families in the 1960's and 1970's.

In addition to a strong desire to be online, just the act of being an observer on social media provides an opportunity to watch what's going on without interacting and become a silent onlooker. On-line, you can interact but still remain anonymous or even pretend to be someone else. This anonymity seems to feed the excitement for many net users. This is illustrated by the famous New Yorker cartoon of a dog sitting at a computer, observing that when he's on the Internet... no one knows he's a dog! For many youngsters, however, even moderately secretive activities may result in social and emotional tensions.

NOTE TO PARENTS WHO ARE CONCERNED ABOUT THEIR KIDS' BEHAVIOR AND SAFETY WHILE ENGAGED IN SOCIAL MEDIA: Parents are concerned about how their youngsters represent themselves on social media and if the anonymity of the web encourages their lack of inhibition. There is abundant advice for both teens and their parents about navigating social media on the web and a good place for families to begin these important conversations. Dr. Larry Magid, an expert on technology and the Internet is a founder of CONNECT SAFELY (CONNECTSAFELY.org) a site with excellent advice and safety materials for families.

Connect Safely offers advice to teens on safe social networking:

http://www.connectsafely.org

1. **"Be your own person**. Don't let friends or strangers pressure you to be someone you aren't. And know your limits. You may be internet savvy, but people and relationships change, and unexpected stuff can happen on the internet.

2. **Be nice online**. Or at least treat people the way you'd want to be treated. People who are nasty and aggressive online are at greater risk of being bullied or harassed themselves. If someone's mean to you, try not to react, definitely don't retaliate, and talk to a trusted adult or a friend who can help. Use privacy tools to block the meanies.

3. **Think about what you post**. Sharing provocative photos or intimate details online, even in private emails, can cause you problems later on. Even people you consider friends can use this info against you, especially if they become ex-friends.

4. **Passwords are private**. Don't share your password even with friends. It's hard to imagine, but friendships change and you don't want to be impersonated by anyone. Pick a password you can remember but no one else can guess. One trick: Create a sentence like "I graduated from King School in 15" for the password "IgfKSi15."

5. **Read between the "lines."** It may be fun to check out new people for friendship or romance, but be aware that, while some

people are nice, others act nice because they're trying to get something. Flattering or supportive messages may be more about manipulation than friendship or romance.

6. **Don't talk about sex with strangers.** Be cautious when communicating with people you don't know in person, especially if the conversation starts to be about sex or physical details. Don't lead them on – you don't want to be the target of a predator's grooming. If they persist, call your local police or contact CyberTipline.com.

7. **Avoid in-person meetings.** The only way someone can physically harm you is if you're both in the same location, so – to be 100% safe – don't meet them in person. If you really must get together with someone you "met" online, don't go alone. Have the meeting in a public place, tell a parent or some other solid backup, and bring some friends along.

8. **Be smart when using a cellphone**. All the same tips apply with phones as with computers. Be careful who you give your number to and how you use GPS and other technologies that can pinpoint your physical location.

9. **Don't measure your own life based on what others post**. People typically post happy photos and stories online and don't usually share their boring or sad moments or unflattering photos. Don't assume that others have better lives than you do, based on what they post."

PHONES FOR EVERYTHING...
BUT TALKING

Children's daily interaction with technology probably begins with a nursery monitor, but quickly their awareness and interests expand. From carefully selected apps and videos to curated child-friendly websites, there comes a day when youngsters graduate to the wireless umbilical cord known as the smart phone. Wireless communications serve a critical role in keeping kids' safe and providing an invaluable family connection. It's comforting that mom is never more than a tap away. But, that's not all.

It seems like everyone is on the phone all the time. Parents give their kids phones so they can be in constant contact when they are away from home. Yet, when children are home, they still stay tethered to their phones. Seeing this, parents may use the opportunity to check their phones, search their e-mail and, perhaps, catch up on some Linked-In posts. Families are together, on their phones, but they are not, necessarily, communicating with each other. This is a fairly accurate picture of how excessive phone use is being modeled and reinforced. Children often cannot get their folks' attention away from their own phones, so they often retreat into social media, gaming and videos. Ultimately, if a parent is able to break this cycle and begin a conversation, "phubbing" or phone snubbing may occur.

Tweens and teens are continuously connected to their phones -- which they use for everything but talking. Most of their phone usage seems to be social media related, monitoring the posts and activities of others and texting, sharing and shaping their digital ID's. Since kids are socializing less in person than ever before, phones are the constant monitor of how one is perceived by others and requires a great deal of attention. Most adults find this vigilant focus on the phone to be exhausting and often rude. But, iGen people comfortably interact with their digital screens, known as phones, as they go about their daily business, in school, during meals and even during the night. In addition, the clarity of their non-verbal conversations is surprisingly good, considering they communicate with a limited vocabulary of emoji's and acronyms, like: OOMF ("One of my followers"), IDK ("I don't know"), RN ("Right now") and ILYSM ("I like you so much")!

Lying in bed, phone in hand, would certainly win the first place ribbon for being the most preferred position and activity on the planet for digital natives. Kids spend countless hours staring at a small digital screen, checking social media, playing games, texting, watching videos, tweeting, doing homework, listening to music, eating and even, sometimes, talking.

For tweens and teens, phones are both appendages and lifelines. Phones can mean continuous connection and acceptance by the group. Phones instruct, remind, entertain, awaken and, importantly, enable socialization. Since 2007, when parents' cell phones morphed into hand-held digital communications centers, kids and their families could message an entire team at once, and conduct lots of other time-saving activities. Kids could take and send selfies and get help with their homework. All while lying on their bed.

Kids now have - in the palm of their hands – the ability to face-time their friends on the other side of town while participating in multi-player games against opponents on the other side of the world. While youngsters wander around this unrestricted public park, they can get lost, stumble or be victimized. Parents hope they can maintain a "walled garden" for their families within this public park, but many adolescents and teens have outsmarted their smart-phone protectors. Even though kids remain snug in their own bedrooms, the challenge for parents is to know where their kids are at all times. Even if they're in a totally virtual place!

The ubiquitous Internet has swept into every aspect of our lives and our iPhone screens are now our most favored appendage. Not only do we use technology to interact with our world, but this technology has become our world and our primary private messenger service. It is this context, thoughts and memories, previously stored in the brain, are conveniently saved and carried in the smart phones of kids and teens. For conscientious parents who have restricted movies by age ratings and controlled adult-oriented cable channels in their homes, there is a disappointing reality about linkages to the Internet. Access to the net means no more virtual safe spaces or safe places -- ever. Smart phones deliver the world-wide web, where you can find everything under the sun. And, your kids probably will!

It would be impossible to quantify all the images and information that circulates through the pixels and channels on the web. As new mobile devises have come on the market, new platforms and websites have expanded, exponentially. The Internet, like a large public park, boasts open spaces for exploring and spreading blankets so groups can come together to picnic and socialize. The net offers stores for buying anything, theatres for seeing anything, schools for learning anything, churches for believing anything and even interactive virtual reality sites where you can experience just about anything.

For many digital natives sleeping with iPhones under their pillows, the pull of their digital content is both constant and compelling. Internet addiction, in my opinion, qualifies as a genuine addiction in the same way that substance abuse or a behavioral disorder can produce compulsive and driven behavior, family stress and disruption of relationships. From rejection to isolation, the connection between depression, "over-thinking" and anxiety and cell phone use of social media seems to be strong.

Regardless of the "why," or other underlying factors that encourage compulsive use of the Internet and the smartphone, people with these habits are often defensive about their behavior. It's important for parents to keep in mind that their children's phones are only, partially, communication tools. Mostly, phones function as computer screens providing non-stop interaction with net-based gaming, social networking and photo-sharing.

GAMING

Gaming is an enormous, multi-billion dollar industry, most of which is driven by the Internet. It's competitive and complicated. The interactive, on-line gaming that occupies young children the most, as well as concerns parents to the greatest degree, is video gaming. Video games engage kids with all the sophisticated bells and whistles of 21st century 3D computer graphics and enticing social connections and customization. Winning is cool, participation and positive reinforcement feel great and being totally engrossed in surreal spaces and other realms brings the brain into a simulated virtual entertainment environment. Mostly, it is the continuous, positive reward that feels good and delivers an immediate, positive punch.

There are numerous positive aspects to game play and its popularity with digital natives cannot be denied. There is research that demonstrates the educational power of games and the remarkable effect that interactivity and learning has on refining motor, cognitive and problem solving abilities. However, the combination of extremely compelling interactivity and the violent content that appears within the story lines of many popular video games has, rightfully, raised the concern and anxiety of parents.

Studies indicate that exposure to certain violent on-line games may exacerbate kids' aggressive behavior and diminish their ability to empathize with others. Although games are officially labeled with appropriate caution by the Entertainment Software Rating Board (ESRB), many "underage" GenZ gamers play these popular adult-rated games.

The category of "first-person shooter" (FPS) games is particularly controversial and raises many red flags for psychologists. These games combine role playing with the ability to interact with, and direct, action on the screen. The individual playing the game takes on the point of view of the story's central character and controls that character's behavior and weapons. In effect, the player can *become* that character! The interactive quality of the game and its continuous reward and feedback cycle is fast and robust. These games, such as Call of Duty and Doom are rapid-paced and, as in other areas of Internet use and addiction, attract and reinforce developing skills. The interaction is powerful as players feel like they are actually experiencing the engagement, a feeling that has significant implications for young, impressionable players.

Exposure to violent content and aggressive play patterns may not be the only safety threats associated with Internet gaming sites. There are also internal risk factors that players may bring to the gaming experience, including their own predispositions to impulsivity and risk-taking. And, exposure to violent behavior simply increases the risk that a child might model that behavior. Many popular gaming platforms do not require any proof of age or offer of monitoring services, like some of the larger social media sites do. Parents must be aware of the fact that their children could encounter various unknown adults while gaming, as well.

NOTE TO PARENTS WHO ARE CONCERNED ABOUT THE EFFECTS OF EXTENSIVE GAMING ON THEIR CHILDREN: The Entertainment Software Rating Board (ESRB.org) provides information and guidance regarding the selection of age and content rated games and apps. ESRB ratings and information helps families and gamers, alike, make age- and skill-appropriate game selections. The ESRB suggests parents check the on all packaged games and determine parental controls for game consoles, mobile, handheld gaming devices. In addition, they recommend that ground rules, including types of content and time restrictions be discussed before play habits take hold. Importantly, parents should monitor other online players in your child's play environment, and report all incidents cyberbullying and profound disrespect.

DON'T BLAME THE MESSENGER: CYBERBULLYING

Before there was cyberbullying, there was just plain bullying. It's important to note that many of the risks we associate with the Internet are not unique to our current, wired world. The threats and dangers that we fear our children may encounter are not new trends in society, either, although they may have intensified with the help of technology. Cyberbullying can be brutal and requires the attention and intervention of caring adults, modeling empathy and standing strong as emotional allies. An important difference with the Internet today is that bullies can operate with anonymity and no risk of retribution, making their deeds even more potent.

Cyberbullying mirrors many of the same negative interactions and issues adolescents and teens experience IRL (in real life). Disparaging and malicious texts and photos - usually based on jealousy, envy or prejudice - are posted on social networks and websites. It has been reported that girls are more likely to be cyberbullied than boys. Boys tend to be more frequent perpetrators than girls, but there are also female perpetrators using social media to harass and humiliate. Illegally obtained and compromised photos or videos, stalking and other hate crimes are considered bullying events that can also have serious legal and law enforcement implications.

Somehow, the off-line world seemed like a far more family-friendly place than the digital environment in which we now live. Back in the day, harassment might have included the passing of an embarrassing picture around to a dozen kids in the school yard. Today, a hundred dozen friends, followers and anonymous onlookers see the picture, share it with even more people and participate in the humiliation. But, the hurtful actions and offensive behavior remains the core bullying message. The harassment, bullying and teasing have been amplified, but not caused by, the Internet.

Before the digital divide, life seemed slower, kinder and easier to manage. The scale was arguably smaller and there were opportunities to erase small mistakes and missteps if one needed to. However, children were still ganged-up upon, humiliated by cliques and even physically harmed. The Internet didn't invent bullying, but it surely has put it on the map. Parents and grandparents must understand that, in the case of bullying, today's cyber technology is simply the messenger.

StopBullying.gov is a government website with information, recommendations and resources for schools and families. The prevention of cyberbullying is critical and it is important for parents to both document and report incidents of repeated cyberbulling and on-line threatening and humiliating postings.

SEXTING AND CYBERSEX

Sexual content and X-rated conversations flow through social media, texts and apps. Skype, FaceTime and Instagram may be popular ways of communicating with grandma, but these digital services are also widely used to relay sexually explicit messages and images. Sexting or talking "dirty" and sharing sexy images also regularly occur on Facetime, Houseparty, Snap, Kik and other digital services and over webcams. Almost any web platform in cyber-space, including gaming, can be used for people to sext, flirt and engage in sexual banter. The common thread among all the messaging is the sexual nature of the content, from conversations to explicit videos.

Also passing through the text services can be erotic poems, jokes and many partial or fully nude images. Sexting sometimes looks like sexy texting, peppered with "for-your-eyes-only" selfies or a range of other compromised photos and X-rated materials. Many of these non-commercial, "personal porn" photographs are original and self-generated. And, the creators may likely be our own own digital natives.

The difference between cybersex and sexting is that cybersex primarily involves a visual sexual act, rather than messages or a conversation about it. Cybersex is often performed live and in real time, using webcams and Skype. Setting the stage for cybersex need not include a hotel room or even being in the same state or the same country with a partner. All that is required are two smart phones with cameras and two participants.

Sexting and cybersex clearly have risks. The smart phone that held a private collection of nude photos, for example, could be exposed, lost, hacked or stolen. Sexts and videos can be passed to others without permission and shared with multiple individuals, media and websites around the globe. Cybersex may begin privately, but often, end publicly. If and when these digital transmissions become public, they can be deeply embarrassing and degrading.

With the help of sophisticated software, some users pixelize their faces or use avatars in order to disguise themselves and remain anonymous on-line. However, protecting private encounters from being forwarded around the web and from hackers, net vultures, extortion and "sextortionists" is extremely complex and often unsuccessful. It is also known that photo sharing need never be revealed to the participant in the photos and could, shockingly, appear years later to great humiliation and, perhaps, sextortion. In addition, sending or even just possessing sexual images of children under the age of 18 is illegal, even if all participants agreed to be photographed. If discovered, those in possession of these pictures could face serious criminal charges for child sexual exploitation. Still, with all of these well-known risks, over half of teens in the U.S. under the age of 18 admit to having sent sexually-oriented messages or photographs over the Internet.

NOTE TO PARENTS WHO ARE CONCERNED ABOUT THE ON-LINE EXPLOITATION OF THEIR YOUNGSTERS:

The National Center for Missing and Exploited Children (NCMEC) is at the forefront of the national conversation on the prevention of child sexual exploitation. NCMEC (www. missingkids.org) operates an extensive website offering advice and information about keeping kids safe on-line. NCMEC facilitates law enforcement's efforts to identify and rescue child victims seen in abusive images on the Internet and operates the CyberTipline, a national reporting system for suspected extortion/sextortion, child molestation and sex trafficking cases.

The National Center for Missing and Exploited Children (NCMEC) and The International Center for Missing and Exploited Children (ICMEC) advocate for the rights and protections of children around the world by providing guidance, support and training to prevent and remove all forms of child exploitation, sexual abuse, abduction and trafficking.

Here are some of their **tips for keeping kids safe on-line:**

http://www.missingkids.com

"**Listen to your children**. Pay attention if they tell you they don't want to be with someone or go somewhere.

Take the time to talk with your children. Encourage open communication and learn how to be an active listener.

Notice when someone shows one or all of your children a great deal of attention or begins giving them gifts.

Talk to your children about the person, and find out why that person is acting in this way.

Teach your children they have the right to say NO to any touch or actions by others that make them feel scared, uncomfortable, or confused and to get out of those situations as quickly as possible. If avoidance is not an option, teach your children to kick, scream, and resist. When in such a situation, teach them to loudly yell, "This person is not my father/mother/guardian," and immediately tell you or another trusted adult.

Reassure them you're there to help and it is OK to tell you anything.

Be sensitive to any changes in your children's behavior or attitude. Encourage open communication, and learn how to be an active listener.

Look and listen to small cues and clues indicating something may be troubling your children because children are not always comfortable disclosing disturbing events or feelings. Some children may not be able to tell because they have been told — by a child molester or exploiter — bad things will happen if they tell what has occurred. Some children may be coerced into activity they didn't at first understand to be inappropriate and/or don't know how to end. Children may be especially fearful of being punished, being embarrassed, or experiencing the loss of the love and respect of their family members and friends.

If your children do confide in you about problems they may be having, strive to remain calm, reassuring, and nonjudgmental. Listen compassionately to their concern, and work with them to get the help they need to resolve the problem.

Be sure to screen babysitters and caregivers. Most jurisdictions have a public registry. Access to and available information about criminal offenses and records varies. Visit www.nsopw.gov, your jurisdiction's registry, or your local law-enforcement agency for specific criteria. Ask your children how the experience with the caregiver was, and carefully listen to the responses.

Provide oversight and supervision of your children's use of computers and the Internet. Know who they're communicating with online and where they may have access to the Internet. Establish rules and guidelines for computer and Internet use for your children.

Be involved in your children's activities. As an active participant you'll have a better opportunity to observe how the adults in charge interact with your children. If you are concerned about anyone's behavior, discuss your concerns with the sponsoring organization."

SEX, LIES AND ON-LINE VIDEO

As far back as the Bible, we've come to understand the natural and, perhaps, biologically driven lure of forbidden fruit. Young iGens are no exception to this phenomenon, as revealed by their predilection for inappropriate and often edgy content on the Internet. Adolescents and teens are wired to take risks. Now, the availability of digital technology allows them to explore all kinds of risky content and stay within the comfort and safety of their own bedroom. They know this ritual because they live in a place filled with pass codes but no zip codes. They live on the Internet.

Life on the net enables post-millennials to create their own virtual identities, and seamlessly integrate their real and virtual worlds. It is through the web and all its extensions and connections that their personal experiences flow. For teens, reality - compliments of technology - is not just a *part* of their identity. It is their identity! These digital natives deal with large amounts of information, real and imagined, as well as utilize the Internet and social media for role modeling, self-invention and reinvention.

From mobile devices to tablets and games, teens rarely communicate with friends unless it's on-line. Whether it's changing relationship status or discussing a character from an streamed episode of a show, the features of the net's 24/7 transmission, going directly into their own private spaces defines this generation. In the tethered world of teens, popularity is validated by likes and followers, but feelings of insecurity are still widespread. Perhaps even more revealing about these kids is the fact that their boundaries for how much they share, and with whom they share, seem fairly indiscriminate.

Possibly, because of lack of face-to-face contact on-line or the rise in impulse-driven social skills, post-millennials tend to excessively communicate and over-share. Social media is the perfect vehicle for endless texting, showing off and bragging. iGen kids are said to be more concerned about what their peers think of them, than what they actually think of themselves. And, attention-yearning Internet personas are created by inventing the person you want to become and then portraying that individual on-line, every day.

GenZ is growing up in an environment where being famous is held in the highest and coolest regard. It almost doesn't matter if it was inspiring or absolutely terrible behavior that thrust a celebrity into social prominence, one can become famous just for being by being famous. Consider Kim Kardashian, the reality TV star, who mentors thousands of young women in the art of fame-making and self-promotion. No one seems to know or care what altruistic or materialistic behavior brought her to prominence in the first place. It's easy to see why self-aggrandizement flourishes in the narcissistic world of Gen Z on social media.

The really famous, not-so famous and probably your child, too, have on-line personas that do not 100% accurately correspond to their authentic selves. Many bios, histories, tweets and posts show embellishments, editing, curating and photo-shopping. In putting their best digital foot forward, iGen members and their Internet stars empower their brand to become their best digital selves. In chat rooms and social networking sites, one can see profiles chocked with fabrications. But not to worry, these virtual personas may be abandoned and then re-invented on a weekly basis.

GenZ members are probably more comfortable and confident with technology than other humans. They chat, play, post, shop and monitor their likes, their sports, their celebrities, friends and frenemies. They claim to know it all and, after consulting with Siri and Alexa, they probably do. For these young adults, the Internet is ground zero for communication and socialization. When they engage with technology, it is immediately apparent that they are wired differently than their parents and just about everyone else from all generations that preceded them. Technology is in their DNA, influencing their relationships, interests and connections to family and friends. Their effortless relationship with all things technical enables them to navigate through a complex maze of electronic data and visual images.

It is impossible to paint all adolescents and teens with one brush, but there are certain developmental traits, like a strong susceptibility to peer pressure, which appear to be a shared characteristic of practically all digital natives. Anyone who remembers junior high can attest to the fact that there are few memories from that time more formidable than the desire to fit in, be popular and be spared rejection. Acceptance by the group is the very basis of the teen dynamic. Of course, even prior to the Internet and on-line communications, adolescents and teens were profoundly concerned about their social status and relationships with peers. Now, with social media, the perfect vehicle for establishing and cultivating social collateral has appeared!

The instant attraction of personalized pictures and videos, coupled with the desire to be noticed, popular and even famous, defines teens' aspirational digital footprint. In the wired world of post-millennials, cool kids are validated by the flaunting of as many friends, contacts and followers as possible. Interestingly, "friend," on the Internet has its own meaning, but is mostly used as a verb describing an outreach to a web acquaintance. Kids are "friended" and "unfriended," with regularity, reminiscent of the game of tag. In general, during the teen years, post-millennials show an increase in virtual friends but a decrease in real-world buds and besties.

Since many youngsters are as emotionally vulnerable as they pretend to be invincible, constant rejection and put-downs can shatter their fragile sense of self-worth. Although it's hard not to feel hurt and rejected when one sees photos of friends participating in parties or activities to which they have not been invited, many of these same youngsters have confessed that they, too, have posted photos intended to be hurtful. This complex scorekeeping between friends, crowds and factions plays out on social media every day. Unfortunately there is a constant audience for what often turns out to be another person's embarrassment or humiliation.

Post-millennials legitimize their existence by tweeting, texting and shouting out their presence to the entire world. Often they will share too much information (TMI) about themselves and their every thought and action. Private contemplations often become public because post-millennials are wired for constant acknowledgment and recognition. In fact, today's adolescents and teens score higher on scales of narcissism than members of all other demographic groups, including previous generations. While everyone would like to have positive recognition and lots of compliments, parents report that their digital natives crave recognition and, in particular, tend to be self-absorbed with feelings of entitlement.

Some narcissistic vulnerability is a normal feature of adolescence and teenage years. Amplified by the web, the need for excessive admiration and entitlement may remain through young adulthood. In terms of demonstrating empathy towards others, iGen members may need help seeing things from the perspective of others and developing empathy and tolerance. Psychologists explain this behavior as the process of "disengagement," when teens try to separate from their parents as they mature. Of course, it is impossible to generalize about a large group of individuals, but we know that teens can be narcissists and may spend hours a day photo-shopping selfies and "improving" stories about themselves and their adventures.

As teens photograph and document every aspect of their lives and themselves on social media, these sharing websites have become a microscope for evaluating their own self-importance. Narcissistic tendencies can emerge as digital natives search the net for a quick fix of recognition and approval by their peers.

NOTE TO PARENTS REGARDING TEEN BEAVIOR ON THE NET:

Teens may, in reality, feel so vulnerable that they act like older, more confident adults, just to feel powerful and important. But, parents should not be fooled. They are, most likely, still just insecure kids in search of necessary guidance. When it comes to life in the virtual world, they need the help and support of their parents, as well as occasional advice. Common Sense Media **(CommonSenseMedia.org),** partners with parents to provide the latest information on technology and media for families with kids of all ages.

Here are Common Sense Media's social media basics for high school kids:

https://www.commonsensemedia.org

"**Think about your online reputation**. Remind teens that anyone can see what they post online -- even if they think no one will. Potential employers and college admissions staff often browse social-networking sites. Ask your teens to think about who might see their pages and how others might interpret their posts or photos.

Anything they create or communicate can be cut, altered, pasted, and sent around. Once they put something online, it's out of their control and can be taken out of context and used to hurt them or someone else. This includes writing as well as photos of sex, drugs, and alcohol. Tell them that online stuff can last forever. If they wouldn't put something on the wall of the school hallway, they shouldn't post it online.

Avoid drama. Don't forward harmful messages or embarrassing photos, and don't impersonate other people by using their accounts or devices or create fake pages.

Don't post your location. Social networks allow kids to post their locations, and, although it might be tempting to use these features to connect with friends or brag about where they've been, it's just not safe for teens.

Watch the clock. Social-networking sites can be real time sucks. Hours and hours can go by, which isn't great for getting homework done, practicing sports or music, or reading."

THE SLIDE INTO INTERNET ADDICTION

Throw out all the stereotypes that you have ever heard about lonely, unhinged kids, sitting in their basements, rejecting school and friends because they are obsessed with the Internet. From soccer-playing teens sleeping with phones under their pillows to honor-roll students huddled with their phones in library cubicles, we're seeing a generation of young people who have more than just a minor interest in life on line. The Internet is always available to the members of GenZ and it always has been. It's conveniently located in the palm of their hands and supports their interaction with school, sports, gaming and dating.

They are constantly learning on the Internet by going deeper and finding out more. The anonymity of the net probably encourages them to find out more, search, explore and drill down more thoroughly than their curious counterparts in previous generations. Of course, this does not mean that exposure, alone, will lead to an addiction, or even a continuing interest. But, with certain vulnerabilities, risk factors and life-style reasons, young digital enthusiasts can generally be led into an even deeper category of Internet use.

The Internet provides the privacy, voluntary control and instant gratification that are the foundation of a pleasure-seeking behavioral addiction. Digital natives are not alone in instinctively wanting to repeat a satisfying encounter that is topped off by a reward. It's natural in the learning process. It's ice cream with the cherry on top. Our memories are quick to trigger the behavior that enables us to repeat a desired activity. The more pleasurable a behavior, the more we want it to recur. Ultimately, the linkages between the behavior and the reward become reinforced. The reward, in this case, is an imperceptible chemical up-tick in the brain. It's a connection that probably transcends the content, itself. Surfing the net and finding what we want actually makes us feel better, as well as personally validated, successful and important.

Traveling down the information super-highway, kids and adults can find forbidden fruit that's tempting and easy to pick. The path from comfort on the Internet - to excessive on-line use - to habitual interaction is a surprisingly unremarkable one. On-line pursuits provide the basis for habits that sometimes become rituals and needs. The journey from clicking through sites to excessive screen time and habitual interaction with those websites is a fairly natural progression. Even occasional Internet users admit to being surprised at the speed with which their casual browsing becomes a looked-forward-to habit. Adolescents and teens, in particular, report a slide into compulsive net-based behavior around interaction with social media and gaming.

Studies have demonstrated that humans are actually biologically prone to getting hooked on searches. The activity of digging and finding the specific content we were looking for on the net can lead to the release of the reward chemical, Dopamine. That combined with other chemicals that rush to the brain, concurrently; create a new reward-center. One can easily see how gaming, searches and social media, accessible on portable devices and available everywhere, can entice vulnerable teens. Attention Deficit Hyperactivity Disorder (ADHD) is considered a predisposing condition and a potential vulnerability to behavioral addictions, including Internet addiction.

Dopamine offers the instant gratification that stimulates an addict's response. Urge-driven disorders, such as gambling and gaming trigger the release of this neuro-chemical and even heighten its subtle kick. Over time, the brain may become dependent on performing this particular behavior in order to receive this satisfying shot of Dopamine. With a smart phone at the ready, an opportunity to wait on line in the cafeteria or sit quietly on the train signals the user to utilize the phone to rereinforce the cycle of addiction.

Long before the web existed, folks understood that the combination of interactivity and personalization felt good and could supply a feeling of satisfaction. Now, we know that the chemistry of the brain responds to the pleasure gained from interacting with the Internet in a similar way. With habitual net-based behaviors, like gaming and gambling there is a feeling of success and "winning". Over time, specific behaviors are invigorated by the disbursement of the reward chemicals in the brain. The build can be rapid or slow, but the satisfaction is very pleasurable and reinforcing.

Behavioral addictions can easily escalate in intensity and rate. When most of us hear the word addiction, we think about illegal drugs and other negative and even life- threatening behaviors. We rarely think that something as ordinary as a daily activity, like being on-line, could become an expectation and an addiction! One tell-tale sign of an addiction is the fact that an individual's tolerance for that activity needs to expand in order to experience the same quality of a "rush" from performing that endeavor. Raising the bar, spending more time, playing increasingly difficult video games and searching for new and novel on-line experiences are often necessary to fulfill the compulsion.

Most educators, medical and social service professionals continue to view excessive Internet usage as a family time-management issue, rather than a potential mental health concern. These professionals rarely use the word addiction to describe compulsive Internet use. The Diagnostic and Statistical Manual of Mental Disorders (DSM), published by the American Psychiatric Association, has issued concerns about Internet "dependency" and "compulsivity." But, it does not categorize excessive Internet usage as an addictive disorder. In fact, the only behavioral (non-substance) addiction that is included in the current DSM is gambling disorder. Dependency is another indication of a habit and can easily be integrated into the cycle of Internet use and abuse. Coupled with emotional problems such as stress, loneliness and anxiety, even moderate Internet use can drive a vulnerable teen deeply into the web to block out negative feelings.

With constant online activity, one might safely assume that many curious kids have encountered inappropriate adult material on the Internet. Parents must come to terms with the reality that it is not a question of *if* their children have been exposed to sexualized content on the net, but only, when. Given the proliferation of sexual and violent programming all over the web and the ubiquity of X-rated videos and films, it is probably very difficult to find normal, computer literate adolescents that have not had even fleeting exposure.

Psychologists have written about the "slide" into risky behavior when one begins experimenting with behaviors previously considered off limits. The model is not a new one. Young teens are still developing the self-regulation abilities to make appropriate and future forward decisions. They are still immature and have not yet tested the social/emotional competencies needed to navigate their way through adult-oriented material. Take checking out pornography on the Internet and envision how you, as a teenager, might handle it:

First comes experimenting when you know isn't right, but, it feels good, it's easy, you are receiving good reinforcement from peers, you're enjoying it, doing it regularly and not getting caught. Since pornography has much the same net-based build as gaming, it becomes a fast-forming ritual. Porn is much easier to come by than drugs or alcohol, making it a perfect "gateway" drug. It invites participation to a wide range of Internet users. You can't flunk it or be rejected by it. And, you don't need money or a driver's license to participate.

Sliding in, you may be doing searches, on-line shopping or link within an e-mail chain. Or, perhaps you end up on a blog that recommends a particular "adult" website. Or, you're looking for the TV show, "Girls", and numerous X-rated websites pop up in front of your eyes! Or it's a totally random and accidental discovery. But after exploring some adult content, a natural curiosity develops.

Sexually oriented Internet videos can be so stimulating that visual memory may absorb and "play" them like a continuous video loop in one's memory. Over and over, these videos can stay in your thoughts and practically highjack your brain with material that is exceptionally arousing. It is hard to turn away. And, if your eyes leave the screen for even a moment, you are compelled to turn back to experience the action, again. This is how it starts.

Like any other gateway drug, searching sexually provocative websites can begin as a one-off activity or even a serendipitous landing on what happens to be a pornography site. Like reading the sports page or keeping up with Facebook friends, visits to these sites can become regular routines and occur increasingly often. When performed habitually, however, these site visits begin to take up a large amount of time and thought-directed energy. They may become an integral part of one's usual daily activity and interfere with other existing patterns of daily life.

Some of these behaviors become integrated into other routines and linked, which can cause additional distress and concern.

Some researchers claim that protracted pornography viewing may encourage preferences for aggressive sexual practices. "Putting your toe in the water," can begin a series of behaviors that signal an increased tolerance for risk. These beginning actions can actually prime the brain to seek out increasing risk. Pornography is considered a gateway drug because it enables the user to explore dangerous situations and to fantasize about everything from infidelity to aggression. It also creates opportunities for participation in increased risk-taking.

NOTE TO PARENTS WHO ARE CONCERNED ABOUT INTERNET ADDICTION:

There are programs and websites dealing with Internet Addiction, sometimes called Internet Addiction Disorder (IAD) and Pathological Internet Use (PIU). Writing for the consumer mental health website, <u>Healthy Place</u> (HEALTHYPLACE. com), Dr. Kimberly Young, advises parents to be aware of addiction signs such as lying, irritability, preoccupation with the Internet, difficulty stopping usage and using the net as a means of coping and escape.

SEX ON THE NET

On large screens and small, seductive photographs and adult videos are downloaded, streamed, posted and watched by teens. One actually doesn't have to look too hard to find sexual material on the net. Even when using the world-wide-web for directions, learning how to apply make-up, playing word games or checking the time and weather, X-rated-websites are just a click away.

There are, of course, enormous differences between your father's PPV Playboy Channel - impossible to view without a credit card, or before 10pm - and the current, easily accessed, 24-7 sexually explicit programing on cable, satellite and YouTube.

There is a proliferation of net-based, sexually explicit content now available at all times of day and night at no cost, via various digital and electronic devises. This has transformed the way kids encounter and consume the adult material we previously considered to be locked away and inaccessible.

The Internet is a powerful influence on youngsters in almost every way, but it is particularly potent on the issue of sexuality. A decade ago, pornographic material may have been confined to VHS tapes that were difficult to purchase or only viewable on a personal computer attached to a telephone line. The Internet is now available and open; and on the open road. With ubiquitous access to everything from explicit photos to hard core pornography, it is not surprising that sexually explicit images have a powerful attraction and impact. Several studies suggest a positive relationship between the age of exposure to sexually suggestive media on the Internet and the age of a youngster's first sexual experience. Although the relationship is not, necessarily, a causal one, exposure and behavior are undeniably linked and the correlation between early viewing of pornography and premature sexual experimentation cannot be denied.

The lure and temptation of sexually explicit pictures and videos, coupled with the intense desire to be accepted and valued by peers, underlies a deep connection for teen users. Building upon a culture of secret messaging, private chat rooms and disappearing snaps, sexualized selfies can become the basis of on-line relationships leveraged around access to a cool and "edgy" adult world. Managing friendships and connections around sexually explicit images and talking and texting about them, contribute to the establishment of a level of comfort and tolerance with other X-rated material. In addition, the secrecy and excitement that surrounds the viewing of sexually explicit material can put enormous pressure on a young person and trigger anxiety about getting caught. iGen guilt over accessing sexually explicit material on the Internet and worry about parental disapproval, punishment or other identification, takes an emotional toll and can result in hyper-vigilant inhibition behaviors.

Early negative encounters watching sex on the net and learning from pornography can sidetrack an individual's entire socialization process. In particular, videos that involve shocking, lewd or sadistic behaviors – or those demonstrating extreme sexual conduct, can cause real confusion, disgust and increased anxiety in young viewers. This exposure, during peak developmental periods such as adolescence, may also prompt future emotional difficulties. This is particularly true when youngsters do not fully comprehend all the actions they are seeing, but are still aroused by viewing those actions.

For some GenZ males, an iPhone loaded with pornographic photos and videos can mean more status than having the followers on Instagram or Vine. Like trading baseball cards in the old days, sending and trading sexual images on the Internet has become a virtual trading clubhouse. A range of sexually explicit images – from the forwarding of slickly produced YouTube productions to intimate, personal cell phone videos are often distributed by teens, themselves. The dissemination of these videos puts these digital natives directly in the porn distribution process.

Post-millennials strive to be as sexually experienced as they assume their peers, friends and frenemies are. There is a lot of posing, showing off and swagger while communicating on-line and sometimes, a social group will create a safe place for this sexting and bragging. In this regard, nervous parents would be well advised not to believe everything they read about their kids on the web.

The quantity of X-rated materials that find their way on to phones, tablets and computers is astonishing. Widely distributed graphic sexual videos as well as personal productions and photo sharing now circulate around the Internet and are often available at low or no cost. Personal porn comprised of home-made photos and videos are a large portion of the YouTube and Internet playbook. The ubiquity of screens, spewing these digital images now surrounds our families with clear, life-like images that are comparable to, if not better than, real life!

Not only are sexualized materials more accessible and widespread than ever, the X-rated content of these materials "push the envelope" to greater degrees that most parents have ever seen. Thousands upon thousands of sexually explicit images and videos are downloaded, aggregated, organized and tagged for showing, sale, sharing and free distribution. In reality, adolescents and teens will likely be exposed to some type of sexual materials even as they innocently explore the Internet using the latest tools.

The underlying potency of all of these sexually explicit images and videos is not their easy accessibility, but their compelling, interactive nature. Compulsive viewing of sexually explicit films and photos could well become a driving force in an individual's life. If it escalates, it can become your life - impacting every aspect of your existence and that of your family. When explicit sexual imagery plays an increasing role in a child's life, parents have the critical responsibility to intervene, provide supportive guidance and control of the flow of these images. The most effective techniques, tools and strategies will be required, as well as a willingness to stay committed to fostering this change.

PORNIFICATION

It has been said that Paris Hilton and Kim Kardashian owe their fame and fortune to less-than-modest videos of themselves widely circulated on the Internet. But, these celebrities have not been shunned, shamed or rejected by society for their behavior. They are, in fact, popular, respected and even admired. How has our society become so pornified?

Like a Trojan horse, pornification moves through a barrage of highly sexualized media. The pull and excitement of pornography stimulates users to seek out more porn and try to find it everywhere. It actually employs the cognitive process called "spreading activation" or searching through existing associations in order to recall information about a particular subject. According to this model, the brain is activated to connect information it has already learned to new material. This activation then prepares or primes the brain to be ready to receive new material. With an enormous library of videos, user generated photographs and websites; it's likely that your post-millennial child is primed and ready for an onslaught of sexually explicit material that will be available to them with the click of a mouse.

As the media continues to sexualize images, young people become primed for an interest in pornography. This interest is intensified by suggestive photos and videos, TV and films and porn websites. The process of "pornification" is an infectious spread of sexually explicit selfies and photographs along with sexualized messages and videos. It moves and inculcates society like a worm working its way through an apple. It quickly digs through layers of culture and values with nothing to stop its path until it seizes your child's iPhone and laptop.

Priming was originally used to describe the preparation of a pump for action. By pouring liquid into a pump, the air would be released and it would pump more efficiently; as in "priming the pump." Now, psychologists use the term, "priming" to include psychological readiness to perform a particular function. Priming can excite and "psych" an individual to be ready for what is coming. So, in addition to digital natives being primed for pornography by a sexualized and pornified culture, there have been startling changes in general acceptance of porn.

In the past, appearing in an X-rated video may have carried a negative stigma within the realm of mainstream entertainment. But, in our increasingly pornified world, porn stars are now the most popular red-carpet celebrities, integrated into the worlds of fashion, television and even politics. But, even though the negative social stigma behind making porn and sex videos has been lifted, there is still embarrassment and shame in communities across the country about using porn. As an activity, unless you are a reality TV star, the pornography business and its excessive use is still considered risky and nasty.

There is little agreement on what porn is or, in reality, what it actually does. We can identify material that is sexually explicit, but we are challenged to explain what, exactly, constitutes obscenity. A photograph of a sexual organ in a medical textbook, for example, is regarded quite differently than a photograph of that same organ on an Internet porn site. The definition of pornography often seems to be in the eyes of the beholder. Naked models in a video designed to elicit sexual arousal meets the general community standard for porn. But, that same video, created by an artist to inspire the viewer's aesthetic sensibility, may be categorized as performance art.

Perhaps Justice Potter Stewart said it best way back in in 1964 when asked for his opinion on obscenity. He admitted to his colleagues on the U.S. Supreme Court that, "I shall not today attempt further to define the kinds of material I understand to be embraced within that shorthand description; and perhaps I could never succeed in intelligibly doing so. *But, I know it when I see it...*"

"Obscenity," is a legal term defined by the U.S. Supreme Court in 1973 to exclude certain sexual content from free speech protections that are secured by the First Amendment of the US Constitution. Fundamentally, the Supreme Court ruled to consider images to be "obscene" if that content appealed to a shared community standard of a high level of indecent or shameful interest in sex; a demonstration of offensive sexual conduct or a sexual demonstration with no cultural, aesthetic or scientific value.

Although not all pornography is obscene, determining the nuanced difference between a pornographic film with artistic "explicit" sexual content and a pornographic film with just "explicit" sexual content is difficult and highly subjective. It highlights the complexity of defining porn and deciding where the line for community standards should be drawn.

It is even more complicated to identify pornographic works from the perspective of a religion or culture. If the U.S. Supreme Court has difficulty defining the nature of sexually explicit images and pornographic material, how easy is it for the rest of us - each of whom looks at the world through their own unique lens of experience? And, how should we determine the level of appropriateness for ourselves and our families without first being exposed to the material and then evaluating our own reactions and levels of comfort?

There is certainly nothing new about pornography, it has been around a long time. Suggestive representations of women and men engaged in sexual encounters go way, way, back, as evidenced by graphic wall drawings in ancient caves. Old legends and mythology are filled with sexual content and illustrations, as Game of Thrones viewers have come to understand. A continuous flow of porn has continued through the centuries and attached to every new technology and delivery system. But, what is new is the virtual interactivity offered by the Internet, combined with ultra-realistic sexual imagery. These authentic, close-up likenesses and the opportunity to practically interact with them, becomes a "perfect storm" for those individuals who are truly vulnerable to porn – and, to porn addiction.

The power of the mobile screen delivery system has, literally, hijacked the Internet and enabled pornography to be available anytime and anywhere. Porn stars are our "A-listers" and sexually explicit material has become the low-hanging and easily accessible forbidden fruit of the new millennium. The increased acceptance of porn today is probably as much a result of our society's tolerance of all things sexual as it is the new era in technology.

The effectiveness of Internet images lie in their personalized content and delivery. An individual's particular proclivities, coupled with the unique effects of this visual stimulus determine how these images are perceived. Erotic videos are often no more than naked actors strutting around in front of a camera. The great fantasy of porn is that it is all a great fantasy. Surely, watching pretty female librarians throw off their glasses and shed their clothes while giving out library cards to muscular men with tool belts is a fantasy which none of us (even Bravo's "Housewives") actually live. Yet, even in its complete silliness, the impact of pornography on our youngsters is dead serious.

PORN HAS CHANGED

Lap-top or lap-dance, today's pornography looks very different from the Playboy Magazine your father stuffed under his mattress. Not only does it look different, but it is more realistic and much more accessible. In the past, viewing porn was covert and costly and it carried a humiliating burden linked to getting caught watching. Now, sexually explicit material is ubiquitous and quickly flowing into suburban homes and workplaces across America.

Just because porn was not created or intended for digital natives and is not, specifically, marketed directly to them, it certainly doesn't mean that they're not watching! Kids don't need to find porn... it finds them. Just about any tween or teen knows what pornography is and that it is just a click away. Many parents are comforted by believing that if their kids don't go looking for porn, it won't find them. What they don't realize, however, is how easily new marketing strategies can push all kinds of content through the web and how the monetization of the web, of "likes" and clicks of even unwitting customers, can actually make money.

The adult film market, home videos and cable television programming have significantly expanded their push of the sexuality envelope onto the Internet. But, for several years, kids have been creating and controlling their own virtual realities, including the sharing of partially clad selfies, nude pictures and sexually explicit videos of themselves and others. Parents should be aware that this personal porn, made by their own kids, is the fastest growing segment of sexually graphic material on the Internet.

Personal porn encompasses the creation and connection of private images. Now, in addition to becoming consumers of X-rated material, the role of creator and distributor of sexually explicit material is not an uncommon one for GenZ. Sexy selfies are being created, viewed, Ogle'd, PhotoSwap'd, kik'd, Meerkat'd and Snap'd in numbers that are both astounding and concerning for parents and families.

It is not uncommon for an iGen boy to ask a female friend to send him a bare breasted selfie as evidence of their friendship or proof of love or interest. It usually comes with a promise that no one else will ever see the picture. It's an alarming trend, grown out of a photo sharing environment in which digital natives seek to gain recognition by documenting every one of their daily activities on social media. Unfortunately, many young women volunteer to share nude or partially nude selfies in order to be better liked and accepted. These images do not always stay exclusive to the recipient.

Once shared and on the web, these pictures can go viral. Photos and videos can easily be linked, texted and e-mailed around the school and even around the planet. Personal pornographic images, from slickly produced YouTube scenes, to intimate personal cell phone videos, enjoy extensive distribution. Forget the sleazy pornographer sitting in a smoke filled room with his feet on a desk sending out dirty pictures and racy e-mails. Some of those gentlemen may still be in business, but personal porn videos are now widely disseminated through free social networks.

INTERNET PORN ADDICTION

Beyond the addictive aspects of returning to the soothing and predictable pleasures of connecting with sexual content, the requirement for porn stimulation does not stay at the same level. The relationship with pornographic material escalates, creating a need for increasingly edgy and riskier material. Like drug addiction, the porn experience does not remain flat and larger quantities or stronger substances are necessary to maintain a satisfactory high. Those in the habit of watching and using pornography often will need increasingly exciting and provocative visuals to stay forcefully engaged. Their desire for highly sexual content will ramp up their Internet searches and explorations.

With porn viewing, this personal on-line interaction continues, but may end with self-stimulation and climaxing to virtual images. Now, the big "win" is not paired with virtual car racing, Angry Birds or on-line poker, but with masturbating to sexually-oriented videos. Perhaps the main reason Internet porn is a problem now, is not a result of technology, but rather of society's tolerance for all things sexual.

When an individual's internalized impulses demand riskier and sexier dosages of porn, we see more time spent with increasingly edgy sexual programming. This includes more jeopardy, better camera angles, more bizarre fetishes and increased action and experimentation. Extending through e-mail, newsgroups, chat rooms and gaming platforms, sexually explicit photographs and videos are distributed throughout the Internet. Addiction to Internet porn is a process that ramps up the amount and sexual edge of the content that is being viewed. Even more significant than access to these visuals is the physical climaxing that often accompanies interaction with that content.

As addiction is reinforced, the thrill of some content wears off and even more stimulating images will be necessary to replace the formerly "satisfactory" high. Ordinary sex in porn may seem dull and the user wants to be stimulated at higher and higher levels. Then, as sexual content becomes increasingly intense, individuals may effortlessly get trapped in an addictive pattern of needing increased stimulation to achieve the same level of satisfaction.

Excessive Internet porn use will, likely, seep into other areas of a young person's life. Guilt, stress and shame, ultimately, build up as dealing with the pressure of keeping porn activities secret demand much of the addict's attention. He may self-medicate through food or working out or even acting out to relieve his stress.

In the beginning of an addiction cycle, users feel energized by the material they have found on the net. At that point, there may be shame about their net escapades, but they probably assume they are already engaging in the behavior with some regularity and have not been caught or experienced any adverse consequences. Once needing to go on line and find more and better visuals, many porn users make up stories and excuses for their behavior and lie to cover up problems with time spent on the Internet. Recurring thoughts about sexual scenarios seen on line may bombard them and risk-taking may interfere with family relationships. A number of behavioral changes may be noticed by family and friends as users try to cover and manage their growing addiction.

Porn hooks because there is an actual biochemical change in the brain that occurs through content repetition and sexual arousal. If the repetition is adequate, these sexual melodramas can take over the brain with material that is exceptionally arousing. Social media sites traffic much of the initial interest for many users. Then, there is an expansion of net-based destinations for those who want to search for even edgier and more sexually explicit material. These searches can become routine, and, eventually evolve into a nightly ritual. It may be only a matter of weeks from the time an obsessive interest in locating and interacting with this material settles into a habit and, ultimately, an addiction.

As addiction creeps in, thinking about porn becomes constant and intense. Along with the cool feeling of "being in the zone" comes excuses and acknowledgements that the individual cannot stop looking at porn. At the same time, however, addicts often feel depressed and frustrated. It's a struggle to remove the addiction by disconnecting the Internet and attempting to end all involvement with daily Internet use. But, without addressing some of the underlying issues that sustain their addiction, relief may only be temporary and relapse is common.

Typically when a young addict stops watching porn, the negative beliefs from feeling sexually inadequate or other emotional problems, pressures and loneliness just come rushing back. Importantly, living in a digital world of Internet connections to almost everything we do, it is extremely difficult to separate from iPhones, computers and the technology that has fostered the habitual porn viewing.

Uncomfortable and distressing images often produce long lasting negative reactions. And, as viewing is repeated, incremental anti-social behaviors are noted. Pornographic and excessively violent depictions, or a combination of both, are particularly problematic. They can become reoccurring thoughts, interfere with sleep and relaxation, and impact both attitudes and behavior.

WHAT PORN REALLY TEACHES

Widespread interest in searching sexual subject matter and exploring virtual pornography on the net has become a global obsession. Porn on the web is available to demonstrate everything you ever wanted to know about sex – and then some, 24-7-365. So, what are our digital natives really learning in the process?

The Internet provides the tangible and physical sensations that link viewers to fantasy. For young viewers this peek becomes a road map and an instructional guide. For teens and adults, sexual arousal unintentionally becomes connected to and dependent upon fantasizing about this virtual image. This fantasy aspect often stays firm, even when viewers are with a "real life" partner. Even years later, close-up images in erotic videos, coupled with the net's gift of interactivity, can place viewers deep within the action.

The smart phone, with its access to the web has made the Internet the "go-to" place for learning about everything sexual. Perhaps the most alarming aspect of the ubiquity of X-rated videos is that GenZ consumers embrace this viewing as an opportunity for authentic learning. Porn should never be a substitute for sex education. But, all too often, it is.

And, when it comes to sex education, porn teaches and reaches. Suggestive videos, erotic photographs, sexting, explicit home-made videos and porn chats will probably reach your children well before you think they are ready. This content is all over the Internet, encouraging unacceptable attitudes and behavior. Invariably, this material reinforces negative stereotypes of women as sex objects and incites undesirable behavior. Unfortunately, however, teens may assume that what they see on- line is informational and accurate regarding sexual practices and norms.

There are millions of graphic sexual images on the Internet which can be accessed by anyone, at any time, from anywhere. Just Google "how to and blank" and you will find a myriad of choices that offer instructions on tasks as varied as how to make French toast to how to take a screenshot on an iPhone or tie a scarf. And, like making French toast, when you are searching for the words, "making love", "sex" and "sexual" you will probably find more instructional information and videos that you will ever have time to watch. In the visual world of virtual images and videos, learning about sex involves hours and hours of learning to have sex. Professional actors as well as your neighbors appearing on YouTube are your instructors.

On and off the Internet, most of us learn by seeing and then, reinforce this learning by doing. This means that anyone on the net, including youngsters, can access stimulating sexual videos, while lying in bed with an iPhone and practically participate in an intimate sexual encounter. Whether commercially produced, available on a YouTube channel or posted by a fellow post-millennial, these images are formidable and crystal clear. With porn so readily available and frequently accessed by young people, it would be naïve to pretend this exposure does not jeopardize the social and emotional wellbeing of our families. Smart phone usage has escalated along with the availability of sexually explicit on-line content, posing potential mental health challenges for our youngsters.

IMPACT OF PORNOGRAPHIC IMAGES

Pornography can manipulate the kind of people we become; how we behave and even what we believe. One would hope that society has evolved past the primitive acceptance of women as sexual objects for the purpose of procreation and survival of the human race. However, the objectification of females is still a reality in society, as well as a prominent part of the X-rated entertainment landscape. Of course, part of the fantasy and illusion of pornography is that it is not like real life. In the non-virtual world, most people wear underwear; don't have bare chested gardeners staring into their kitchen windows or steam showers at the ready in their corner offices. The settings of porn films; lavish hotel rooms and beautiful, deserted beaches are far from the familiar realities of suburbia or the annoying consequences of STD's.

Pornographic films and videos can be so overly staged and dramatic, that they can have the effect of making real sex less satisfying. In reality, most sexual relationships rarely live up to the thrill or excitement seen in porn thereby raising issues of disappointment, not enthusiasm. An important take-away from these videos is that sex is usually seen as a physical exercise and a totally separate entity from emotional connections or loving relationships.

Web-based pornography can have a huge imprint and effect upon a young person. We know that these videos can create an underlying expectation that all sexual experiences will be amazing and "over the top." Unfortunately, these expectations may lead to feelings of inadequacy as well as dissatisfaction. The performance of porn actors furthers this belief and reinforces the way people are "supposed" to behave while making love. These porn performances may remain etched in the minds of viewers, leaving both women and men feeling disappointed and dissatisfied.

As a reaction to viewing, some male adults report disappointment dating women who are not thong-wearing vixens or surgically enhanced Barbie look-alikes. In the case of socially immature individuals, scenes which look like romance novel covers with half clothed women panting in sexual readiness may become aspirational. Obviously, responsible parents will do what they can to prevent their children from seeing explicit videos like this or modeling such behavior.

In examining our values and attitudes, some people will consider an evening with pornography a free pass or a way to experiment watching others have sex while remaining physically and emotionally faithful to their non-virtual partners. But, in a virtual sexual experience, the brain can deceive the viewer into feeling that he has actually participated in a real sexual encounter. Since he will probably react more strongly to things that are new and novel, he will naturally become excited by the unfamiliar. Following exposure to Internet pornography, some men will fantasize about the bra model or hot librarian seen in a video, in order to become sexually aroused during intimate situations with their real-life partners.

For most parents, the level and content of pornography is a major concern. Typically, pornography falls into two sub-categories; softcore and hardcore. Softcore pornography shows individuals who are naked or partially clothed and engaging in sexually suggestive situations, whereas hardcore contains graphic depictions of sexual acts. Today, many of the most popular shows on cable, premium and Internet channels would be considered softcore. Thirty years ago, hardcore porn was difficult to come by. Today, it is readily available on the net. Fortunately, however, much of the commercially-produced extreme hardcore videos are found on paid and restricted (over age 18) websites.

Shockingly, hardcore and violent pornography may be the most effective influencer for sexual abuse and rape in our society. The effects of its content are toxic and can be emotionally contagious. This type of porn sometimes depicts the malicious, age-old storyline of a rape fantasy where a woman is being held down and threatened. Ultimately, she is overcome and the smug take-away is "the lady doth protest too much." This horrific portrayal and rationale for sexual assault is sometimes incorporated into violent porn and has become an entrenched pathology in our culture.

Since the Internet is considered the "go to" sex-educator for youngsters, it is possible that iGen teens could stumble on to this genre of porn. Although viewing does not, necessarily, lead to acceptance, youngsters could easily be influenced towards a lack of compassion and desensitized to the real horrors of rape and sexual assault. For impressionable adolescents and teens, discovering this type of porn, is very risky.

Parents worry about all types of addiction. But, it's important to note that unlike addiction to nicotine or even drugs or alcohol -- which will, ultimately, be excreted from the physical body -- pornographic images may remain in memory forever. The brain is a repository of information that never leaves us. Sometimes, intrusive thoughts do pop-up, unexpectedly. These images, captured in our brains via media and the Internet, can remain with us for a very long time. Now is the time for us to join together and create a safe digital environment for all of our families. We should accept nothing less.

REVENGE PORN AND SEXTORTION

Revenge porn is not always motivated by revenge and it isn't, necessarily, always considered pornographic. The public sharing of pictures or videos for the purpose of embarrassing or shaming the sexually compromised person featured is legally considered non-consensual pornography. Regardless of the fact that the original images were obtained voluntarily or recorded secretly, hacked or even stolen, it's one of the more dangerous aspects of teen texting and sexting. Through private photo sharing, compromised images of an identifiable person might be seen and spread, without their knowledge. It can happen immediately after a boyfriend agrees to keep the images private or years later in an unintentional data dump.

The practice of the public sharing of identifiable compromised photographs or videos for the purpose of spite or humiliation is bad enough. But now, a number of revenge porn and other victims have reported being "sextorted" (extorted for money, additional photographs or even sexual favors) by the individuals who have stolen or hacked these photographs and threatened to distribute them further. This very serious form of blackmail and photo dissemination underscores how dangerous this issue can become. An adolescent's immature behavior or topless selfie could, potentially, be immortalized forever and cause terrible distress over an entire lifetime.

Although it varies by state, a revenge porn victim over the age of 18 can proceed, legally, against the person who distributed compromised images of her, but it is difficult and costly. And regardless of any potential penalty, or even if the image removed from a revenge porn website, the photo can still be forwarded from another source seeking maximum mean-spirited vengeance or to a college selection committee or potential employer. There have been cases where 18-year-olds have forwarded nude photos of their former under-age girlfriends and were later charged as sex offenders. A "selfie" of a 16-year-old may be considered child pornography under the law.

NOTE TO PARENTS WHO ARE CONCERNED ABOUT THE EXPLOITATION OF THEIR YOUNGSTERS ON THE NET:

The National Center for Missing and Exploited Children (NCMEC.org) is our national clearinghouse for issues related to the sexual exploitation of children. NCMEC now monitors "sextortion" a growing problem on the Internet where children and their families may be threatened or even blackmailed in exchange for keeping sexually compromised photos and videos private. Here are some of the tactics sextortionists are using:

How is sextortion is occurring?

http://www.missingkids.org

Many different manipulation tactics were used by offenders, often in combination, to achieve their apparent objectives. The most common tactic that reporters indicated were the offender threatening to post previously acquired sexual content online (67%) and, often, specifically threatening to post it in a place for family and friends to see (29%) if the child did not comply.

Other tactics used by the offenders include:

Reciprocation, whereby the offender coerced the child into providing sexual content by promising reciprocity ("I'll show you if you show me")

Developing a bond by establishing a friendship/romantic relationship

Secretly recording sexually explicit videos of the child during video chats

Physically threatening to hurt or sexually assault the child or family members

Using multiple online identities against a given child, such as the person blackmailing for sexual content as well as pretending to be a supportive friend or a sympathetic victim of the same offender

Pretending to be younger and/or a female

Accessing the child's online account without authorization and stealing sexual content of the child

Threatening to create sexual content of the child using digital-editing tools to merge the child's face with another person's body

Threatening to commit suicide if the child does not provide sexual content

Creating a fake profile as the child and threatening to post sexual content of the child

Initially offering something to the child, such as money or drugs, in exchange for sexual explicit photos/videos

Pretending to work for a modeling agency to obtain sexual content of the child

Saving sexually explicit conversations with the child and threatening to post them online

While the majority of these manipulation tactics were used equally against male and female children, there were significant differences in the use of certain methods. More specifically, when child victims were male, offenders were significantly more likely to pretend to be younger and/or a female, offer to engage in sexual reciprocity through shared images or by live-streaming, record the child unknowingly and then threaten to post the images/videos so family and friends could see. In contrast, when child victims were female, offenders were significantly more likely to offer something to get initial sexually explicit content from them, such as money or drugs.

NET-BASED SEXUAL EXPLOITATION

According to the Office of Justice Programs (OJP), children and teens are extremely vulnerable to becoming victims of Internet crimes. Teen girls are the most susceptible of all. Predators use the net to reach out to young people, with a general purpose of engaging them in relationships that might, one day, move off line. On-line predators will encourage their young prey to send and exchange photos of themselves as well as porn.

A pedophile is an adult predator with sexual desires towards prepubescent children. The American Psychiatric Association (APA) has classified this intense attraction as a psychological disorder, listed in the Diagnostic and Statistical Manual of Mental Disorders (DSM-5). These individuals often find legitimate ways to be around kids and may have long term relationships with families of children in whom they have a sexual interest or are even members of these extended families. There is frequently a justifiable reason for their relationship with a particular child, either as a coach, neighbor, and member of the clergy, teacher or babysitter. Rarely, are these individuals considered actual strangers or frightening individuals to their child victims. The process that pedophiles use to become liked and trusted by their victims is called grooming. They mentor and prime the specific children they find of interest, participate in their activities and connect with their friends and families.

A common off-line predatory practice is rough play, wrestling and horsing around. Pedophiles often do a lot of playful touching in public to legitimize some of the secret touches and physicality they want to recreate when they are in a private setting with a youngster. Horsing around and even "torture tickling" may start out as fun but can also become aggressive and sexual. Sometimes, it is used to provide cover for inappropriate touching.

Regardless of how the predator originally meets and grooms his victims, the Internet is his most strategic means of priming his victim. The net offers non-parent-mediated direct digital access through public channels of communication. Disappearing texts sent on Telegram, Snap, Wicr, Hash or StealthChat are part of the outreach repertoire that predators use. These individuals may even purchase e-mail addresses from agencies aggregating web data from kids' birthday club memberships, cheerleading competitions and school couponing. Not surprisingly, there are net-based social communities for people with this disorder where they swap photographs and discuss their common anti-social interests.

Viewing and sharing pornography and social media chats may be the main focus of a pedophile's activity on the Internet. It is also not uncommon for an individual with these sexual inclinations to use pornographic material to lower his victim's sexual inhibitions and lure them into a sexual encounter. Both heterosexual and homosexual men are equally likely to become pedophiles and many people with the disorder have a history of sexual abuse in their own past.

Pedophiles are often manipulative individuals and smooth operators at finding children's natural vulnerabilities, such as their desire to be treated as special and older. The pedophile will also offer attention, money, gifts, affection and the sharing of secrets to gain trust and appreciation. By playing on a youngster's emotions and insecurities, ultimately, the predator wants to persuade the child to have a private encounter, and will patiently wait until the child is ready. Courting and priming potential prey on-line usually includes virtual associations with shared interests such as sports, multi-player video games and collecting.

The Innocent Images National Initiative (IINI) is a unit of the FBI tasked with catching and prosecuting pedophiles. IINI looks exclusively at the Internet priming and luring of potential victims, in Internet news groups, child porn sites, Internet Relay Chats (IRC), forums and social media sites. Since the enticement of kids on-line has become the pedophile's preferred means of connecting with children, parental oversight of all web activities involving kids is critical. According to my friend and former Fox colleague, John Walsh, child safety advocate and host of TV's America's Most Wanted and The Hunt with John Walsh, "These are no longer the days of Father Knows Best. These are tough days. Now the predators are not just driving up and down the street, they're in your living room on the Internet."

ABOUT THE AUTHOR

Who better to lead a national conversation about the impact of technology and media on kids and their families than Dr. Helen Boehm? She is a distinguished psychologist who leads the independent advisory, **FCC Ready**, which certifies educational television programming to be in compliance with Federal Communications Commission standards and consults with media and technology companies and governmental and educational organizations on the development of digital products, policies and services.

Dr. Helen served as Viacom's MTV Networks/Nickelodeon Senior Vice President for Public Responsibility and Standards and headed Public Service and Kid's Practices at the Fox Broadcasting Company. A familiar parenting resource on TV and the net, she has been a spokesperson for the Toy Industry Association, VTech and the advertising industry's Children's Advertising Review Unit (CARU). Dr. Helen has given expert testimony on media and advertising in front of the U.S. Congress and is the author of the popular trade paperbacks, The Right Toys: A Guide to Selecting the Best Toys for Children and Fearless Parenting for the New Millennium. A mother and grandmother, she is a graduate of Boston University and received masters and doctoral degrees from Columbia University.

Printed in the United States
By Bookmasters